This book
belongs to:

LEISURE ARTS, INC.
Little Rock, Arkansas

EDITORIAL STAFF

Editor-in-Chief: Anne Van Wagner Childs. *Executive Director:* Sandra Graham Case. *Executive Editor:* Susan Frantz Wiles. *Publications Director:* Carla Bentley. *Creative Art Director:* Gloria Bearden. *Production Art Director:* Melinda Stout. PRODUCTION — *Managing Editor:* Susan White Sullivan. *Senior Editor:* Carla A. Jones. *Project Coordinators:* Stephanie Gail Sharp and Andrea Ahlen. DESIGN — *Design Director:* Patricia Wallenfang Sowers. EDITORIAL — *Associate Editor:* Linda L. Trimble. *Senior Editorial Writer:* Tammi Williamson Bradley. *Editorial Associates:* Terri Leming Davidson, Robyn Sheffield-Edwards, and Darla Burdette Kelsay. *Copy Editor:* Laura Lee Weland. ART — *Book/Magazine Art Director:* Diane M. Ghegan. *Senior Production Artist:* Stephen L. Mooningham. *Production Artist:* Mark A. Hawkins. *Art Assistants:* Hubrith E. Esters and Deborah Taylor. *Photography Stylists:* Christina Tiano, Karen Hall, Sondra Daniel, and Laura Bushmiaer. ADVERTISING AND DIRECT MAIL — *Senior Editor:* Tena Kelley Vaughn. *Copywriters:* Steven M. Cooper, Marla Shivers, and Jonathon Walker. *Designer:* Rhonda H. Hestir. *Art Director:* Jeff Curtis. *Artist:* Linda Lovette Smart. *Typesetters:* Cindy Lumpkin and Larry Flaxman.

BUSINESS STAFF

Publisher: Steve Patterson. *Controller:* Tom Siebenmorgen. *Retail Sales Director:* Richard Tignor. *Retail Marketing Director:* Pam Stebbins. *Retail Customer Services Director:* Margaret Sweetin. *Marketing Manager:* Russ Barnett. *Executive Director of Marketing and Circulation:* Guy A. Crossley. *Fulfillment Manager:* Byron L. Taylor. *Print Production Manager:* Laura Lockhart. *Print Production Coordinator:* Nancy Reddick Lister.

CREDITS

PHOTOGRAPHY: Ken West, Mark Mathews, and Karen Busick Shirey of Peerless Photography, Little Rock, Arkansas; and Jerry R. Davis of Jerry Davis Photography, Little Rock, Arkansas. COLOR SEPARATIONS: Magna IV Color Imaging of Little Rock, Arkansas. CUSTOM FRAMING: Nelda and Carlton Newby of Creative Framers, North Little Rock, Arkansas. PHOTO LOCATIONS: The homes of Holly Curry, Nancy Gunn Porter, Frank and Carol Clawson, Sandra Cook, John and Anne Childs, Shirley Held, Carl and Monte Brunck, and Linda Wardlaw.

Library of Congress Catalog Number 94-76794
International Standard Book Number 0-942237-40-4

INTRODUCTION

In each budding flower, clear blue day, ripening field, and glistening snowfall, the splendor of the changing seasons reflects nature's artistry. Just as we are today, the Victorians were delighted by the beauty of the four seasons. An antique calendar with scenes from every season inspired us to create this book of timeless cross stitch for you to enjoy all through the year. Many of the idyllic designs that accompany these four masterpieces are reproductions of artwork that we discovered on old-time postcards and other turn-of-the century memorabilia. In Seasons Remembered, you'll not only find projects that celebrate the year's natural wonders, but also designs to mark the special events and activities associated with them. There's a birth announcement to welcome a newborn and a wedding sampler for the June bride. For the time of thanksgiving, a serving tray makes a lovely accent, and shimmering flakes fall on warming winter apparel. As you browse through the following pages, may you experience the promise and anticipation of spring's floral offerings, the pleasures of summer's long and lazy days, the beauty of autumn's changing foliage, and the enchantment of a wintry wonderland.

TABLE OF CONTENTS

WINTER

There's something magical about a dusting of powdery white snow that brings out the child in each of us. While cottony soft flakes float to the ground, a sense of anticipation builds as we prepare for the frosty fun of making snowmen, sledding down the hillside, and catching snowflakes on our tongues. Bundled in warm woolen layers, we brave winter's chill for the chance to dance beneath falling flakes and watch angels appear in the snow. This season of icicles and enchantment brings many reasons to venture outside, but when you choose to stay indoors by the fire, our heartwarming collection offers an abundance of wintry designs for you to enjoy.

Chart on pages 48-49

Let the North Wind blow —
you'll be toasty warm in these cold-
weather fashions! Embellished with
beaded snowflake motifs, a pretty
sweater reflects winter's icy beauty. A
sprinkling of snowy accents makes
a scarf and mitten set ideal accessories
for outdoor fun. 'Neath a wreath of
mistletoe, a blushing miss bestows
a kiss upon her frosty pal.

Chart on page 57

Chart on page 57

Chart on page 53

A blanket of powdery snow provides an ideal winter playground. Reflecting the outdoorsy spirit, a black-on-red alpine design gives a sweatshirt masculine appeal. In a vintage Currier and Ives scene, a handsome couple enjoys a brisk sleigh ride.

Chart on page 57

Chart on pages 50-51

Chart on page 52

Chart on page 57

ℏandmade accents like these lend a cozy touch to your winter decor. The cheery song of a feathered friend can chase away the chill from a snow-frosted day, and the love of home and a snuggly wrap are winter warmers like no other.

Charts on page 56

15

But give me the holly, bold and jolly,
Honest, prickly, shining holly;
Pluck me holly leaf and berry
For the day when I make merry.

— *CHRISTINA ROSSETTI*

Chart on pages 54-55

Charts on pages 54 and 55

With its vivid berries and glossy leaves, holly spreads vibrant color over the snowy countryside. A spray of ribbon-tied holly makes this sweater ideal for day or evening wear. Captured on classic table linens, sprigs of holly lend elegance to formal dining, and a coordinating design brings seasonal cheer to a cozy throw pillow.

Chart on page 54

SPRING

As its gentle breezes and caressing warmth unfold around us, spring fills us with a sense of anticipation and promise. Each budding tree and greening field makes us think again of childhood days, when a simple clover chain was a priceless adornment and we whiled away the hours playing youthful games. Gathering baskets of fragrant wildflowers, we accept spring's colorful invitation to bring its delicate aromas indoors. May this nostalgic collection refresh your appreciation for the season of renewal.

Chart on pages 58-59

Chart on page 60

Chart on page 61

Spring flowers are a welcome sight wherever they bloom. Adorning the collar of a plain blouse, a sweet nosegay adds a feminine touch. A flowering bough offers a safe and gentle cradle for a nest of tiny eggs.

Chart on page 61

Chart on page 63

Exploring the awakening countryside is one of the joys of springtime. Our young miss spies a pretty butterfly and discovers that she's not the only one enchanted by the rainbow of color in a field of wildflowers. A pair of tiny birds perched on a flowering branch offers an early-morning song as a pleasant wake-up call to the new day.

Chart on pages 66-67

Charts on page 62

With a profusion of life and color, the advent of spring stirs nature from its perennial slumber. A nest of robin's eggs rests among pretty pink flowers — a lovely reminder that this is the season of renewal. Vibrant daffodils and irises transform sachets and a bookmark into thoughtful tokens of friendship.

Cherish this Child

Robert Sidney Griffith

A Gift from God to:
Katherine & William Griffith

Born on this Day:
November 29, 1995

Chart on pages 64-65

*C*elebrate a new arrival with precious gifts. A cherubic trio commemorates the blessed event on a sweet birth announcement. Lovingly collected in a porcelain jar, baby's special keepsakes mark the passage of time. The curiosity of a child adds joy to the simple pleasures of life.

Chart on page 64

Chart on page 66

SUMMER

Lazy summer days entice us out-of-doors to enjoy nature's peace and beauty. As fluffy white clouds promenade across a bright blue sky, it's easy to forget our cares and indulge in an idle hour of daydreams. Or perhaps, like this fair maiden, we could slip away to a meadow and lose ourselves in the pages of a favorite novel. In this collection, you'll find a myriad of inspirations for enjoying a sunny summer afternoon.

Chart on pages 68-69

For mine is just a little old-fashioned garden where the flowers come together to praise the Lord and teach all who look upon them to do likewise.

— CELIA THAXTER

Chart on page 75

Chart on page 74

Charts on pages 75 and 78

*C*oaxed forth by the sun's warming rays, a bountiful summer garden pays tribute to the gardener's diligent care. An assortment of old-fashioned seed packets inspired colorful plant pokes, pillows, and a shirt pocket accent. Matching border designs add just-picked freshness to kitchen towels.

Charts on pages 80 and 81

Charts on page 79

I watch my garden beds after they are sown, and think how one of God's exquisite miracles is going on beneath the dark earth out of sight. I never forget my planted seeds.

— CELIA THAXTER

Chart on page 80

Charts on pages 80 and 81

33

Chart on pages 70-71

Charts on page 77

The sandy shores of the great blue sea are adventure-lands for young and old alike. Along endless beaches we collect shells and watch for ships sailing along the horizon. Here, with its eternal ebb and tide, the water inspires dreams of faraway lands and things that are yet to be.

Sea Fever

I must down to the seas again,
  to the lonely sea and the sky,
And all I ask is a tall ship
  and a star to steer her by,
And the wheel's kick
  and the wind's song
  and the white sail's shaking,
And a grey mist
  on the sea's face
  and a grey dawn breaking,
I must down to the seas again,
  for the call of the running tide,
Is a wild call and a clear call
  that may not be denied.

John Masefield

Chart on pages 76-77

Two Hearts
One Love
Today and Always

Patti & Jimmy
6·25·94

Chart on pages 72-73

Chart on page 72

Tokens of affection help us celebrate special days and strengthen the ties of love. A beaded wedding sampler is a cherished gift for a June bride. Fragrant sachets evoke sweet thoughts of romance, and a delicate pillow is a lovely accent.

Chart on page 73

AUTUMN

Crisp, cool days and a spectacular showing of glorious fall foliage welcome the arrival of autumn. During this colorful time, when the rustling leaves seem to beckon us outside, we delight in renewing familiar customs like gathering pumpkins to adorn our homes or taking an evening hayride. Giving thanks for the season's harvest is a tradition we've celebrated since the Pilgrims first settled in this great country. The designs in this collection, like the brilliant leaves of autumn, offer a cornucopia of rich color that invites us to pause and reflect on the beauty of the season and count our blessings.

Chart on pages 82-83

Chart on pages 84-85

Autumn's cooler weather ushers in a taste for hearty breads and a sampling of homemade jams. Fresh from the oven, rolls, loaves, and muffins stay warm and delicious wrapped in cozy bread covers bearing fruity motifs. Coordinating designs also top jars of tasty jellies and preserves.

Charts on page 90

heap high the board with plenteous cheer, and gather to the feast,
And toast the sturdy Pilgrim band whose courage never ceased.
Give praise to that All-Gracious One by whom their steps were led,
And thanks unto the harvest's Lord who sends our "daily bread."

— ALICE WILLIAMS BROTHERTON

Chart on pages 86-87

Chart on pages 86-87

45

Chart on page 89

Chart on page 91

*T*he glories of autumn include a splendid display of color that blazes across the countryside. More subtle, but no less beautiful, is the occasional sighting of a flock of migratory birds gathered beside a quiet pond. Bring the beauty indoors with an accent pillow created in russets and golds, or adorn novel bookmarks with children dressed in old-fashioned attire.

Charts on page 88

X	DMC	¼X	¾X	½X	B'ST
−	ecru				
▨	* 351 & 3778	◿			
C	352	◿			
	353	◿			
+	* 353 & 760				
▲	355	◿			
⊙	356	◿		▣	◿ †
▨	* 356 & 355	◿			
✦	407			▣	
	415			☆	
■	640	◿		⊙	
	645	◿			
5	646	◿			
	647	◿		▢	◿ ★
△	648				
✳	729	◿			
	754	◿			
	758	◿	□		
4	760				
V	761				
	762			⊙	
■	816	◿			
	827			◆	
	839	◿			
3	840	◿		4	
⊙	841	◿			
☆	842	◿			
✖	844	◿			◿ ▲
	932	◿		◆	
□	948	◿			
2	950	◿		N	
R	3022	◿			
C	3023	◿			
+	3024			▣	
■	3031	◿			
⊙	3032	◿		✖	
4	3045	◿			
	3064	◿			
✿	3328	◿			
S	* 3328 & 347	◿			
★	3371	◿			◿
	3712	◿			
	3772	◿			
	3774			S	
H	3778	◿			
V	3781	◿			◿ ★
−	3782	◿		⁑	
▲	3787	◿			◿ ▲
C	3790	◿		R	◿ ▲

Blue area indicates first row of right section of design.

* Use 2 strands of first floss color listed and 1 strand of second floss color listed.

† Use 2 strands for mouths.

★ Use 647 for snow. Use 3781 for eyes and eyebrows.

▲ Use 844 for rope. Use 3787 for tree. Use 3790 for fence.

STITCH COUNT (116w x 116h)

14 count	8⅜"	x	8⅜"
16 count	7¼"	x	7¼"
18 count	6½"	x	6½"
22 count	5⅜"	x	5⅜"

Winter Fun in Frame (shown on page 9): The design was stitched over 2 fabric threads on an 18" square of Antique White Lugana (25 ct). Three strands of floss were used for Cross Stitch and 1 strand for Half Cross Stitch and Backstitch, unless otherwise noted in the color key. It was custom framed.

Needlework adaptation by Nancy Dockter.

X	DMC	¼X	¾X	½X	B'ST
	blanc				
	310				
	318				*
	319				
	320				
	353				
	353 & 760				
2	355				
	356				
	367				
	413				
	414				
4	415				
–	422				
	520				
	611				★
*	612				
S	645				▲
	646				
	647				
C	648				
	680				°
	754				
	758				
O	762				
★	839				★
	844				
	930				*
	931				
	932				
◊	948				
3	3021				★
	3031				
	3045				°
4	3051				
	3072				
☆	3328				
	3328 & 355				
	3371				▲
*	3712				
	3750				
	3781				
	3790				
	3799				
	3820				
△	3822				

Blue area indicates first row of right section of design.

* Use 318 for house. Use 930 for tie.

† Use 2 strands of first floss color listed and 1 strand of second floss color listed.

★ Use 611 for grass. Use 839 for eyebrows, eyes, and gloves. Use 3021 for trees.

▲ Use 645 for house. Use 3371 for hair.

° Use 680 for sleigh. Use 3045 for grass.

Sleigh Ride in Frame (shown on page 13): The design was stitched over 2 fabric threads on a 20" x 16" piece of Confederate Grey Cashel Linen (28 ct). Three strands of floss were used for Cross Stitch and 1 strand for Half Cross Stitch and Backstitch. It was custom framed.

Needlework adaptation by Nancy Dockter.

STITCH COUNT (162w x 109h)

14 count	11⅝"	x	7⅞"
16 count	10⅛"	x	6⅞"
18 count	9"	x	6⅛"
22 count	7⅜"	x	5"

I heard a bird sing
In the dark of December
A magical thing
And sweet to remember.

"We are nearer to Spring
Than we were in September."
I heard a bird sing
In the dark of December.
Oliver Herford

December Songbird in Frame (shown on page 14): The design was stitched over 2 fabric threads on a 15" x 16" piece of Cream Quaker Cloth (28 ct). Three strands of floss were used for Cross Stitch and 1 strand for Backstitch and French Knots, unless otherwise noted in the color key. It was custom framed.

Design by Donna Vermillion Giampa.

STITCH COUNT (90w x 100h)

14 count	6½"	x 7¼"
16 count	5⅝"	x 6¼"
18 count	5"	x 5⅝"
22 count	4⅛"	x 4⅝"

X	DMC	¼X	B'ST
✶	310		
	351		
4	352		
★	500		
⊙ *	502		
2 *	503		
− *	504		
◆	561		
V	562		

X	DMC	¼X	B'ST
□	564		
■ †	645 & 817		
◆ †	647 & 351		
▦ †	648 & 352		
✸	666		
S	741		

X	DMC	¼X	B'ST
	742		
■	814		
	817		
	902		
✦	3031		
	3032		
3	3046		
△	3047		
	3072		

X	DMC	¼X	B'ST
C †	3072 & 353		
	3345		
■	3346		
X	3347		
4	3348		
5	3782		
S	3790		
●	500	French Knot	

X	DMC		
⊙	3072	French Knot	

* Use 1 strand of floss.
† Use 2 strands of first floss color listed and 1 strand of second floss color listed.

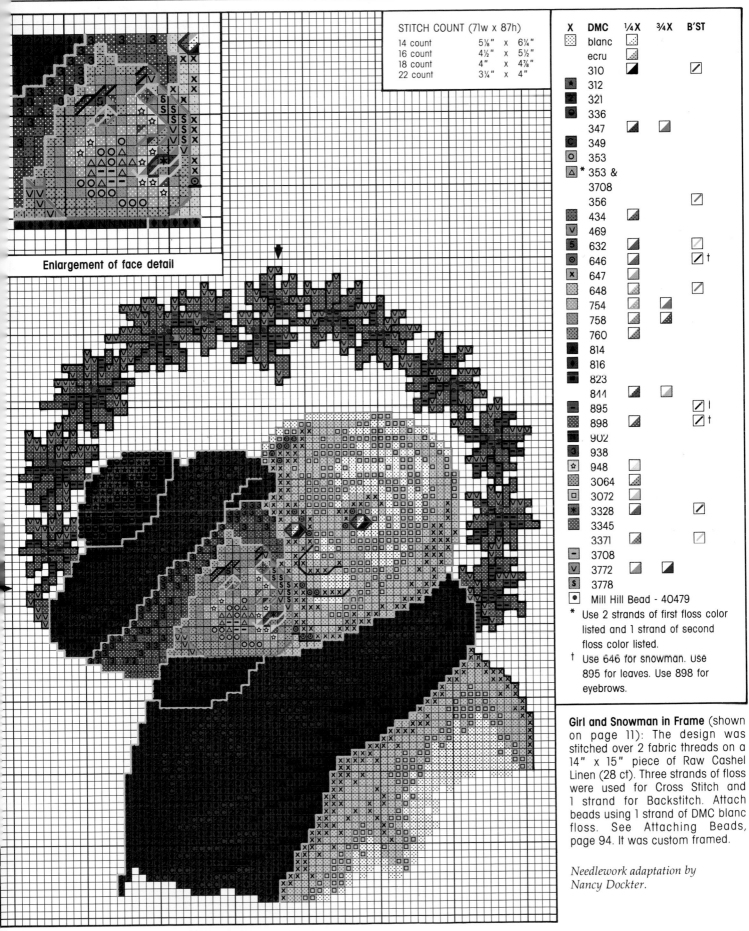

Enlargement of face detail

STITCH COUNT (71w x 87h)

14 count	5⅛"	x	6¼"
16 count	4½"	x	5½"
18 count	4"	x	4⅞"
22 count	3¼"	x	4"

X	DMC	¼X	¾X	B'ST
▦	blanc	▦		
	ecru	▦		
	310	◣		◿
✦	312			
▨	321			
◉	336			
	347	◣	◣	
▣	349			
◎	353			
△	* 353 &			
	3708			
	356			◿
▦	434	◣		
V	469			
5	632	◣		◿ †
◉	646	◣		◿ †
✕	647	◣		
▨	648	◣		◿
▨	754	◣	◣	
▨	758	◣	◣	
▨	760	◣		
■	814			
◆	816			
▬	823			
	844	◣	◣	
−	895			◿ I
▨	898	◣		◿ †
◧	902			
⅃	938			
☆	948	◻		
▨	3064	◣		
◻	3072	◣		
✳	3328	◣		◿
▨	3345	◣		◿
▨	3371	◣		◿
−	3708			
V	3772	◣	◣	
S	3778			
●	Mill Hill Bead - 40479			

* Use 2 strands of first floss color
listed and 1 strand of second
floss color listed.

† Use 646 for snowman. Use
895 for leaves. Use 898 for
eyebrows.

Girl and Snowman in Frame (shown
on page 11): The design was
stitched over 2 fabric threads on a
14" x 15" piece of Raw Cashel
Linen (28 ct). Three strands of floss
were used for Cross Stitch and
1 strand for Backstitch. Attach
beads using 1 strand of DMC blanc
floss. See Attaching Beads,
page 94. It was custom framed.

*Needlework adaptation by
Nancy Dockter.*

WINTER

#1 (132w x 55h)

#2 (93w x 66h)

54

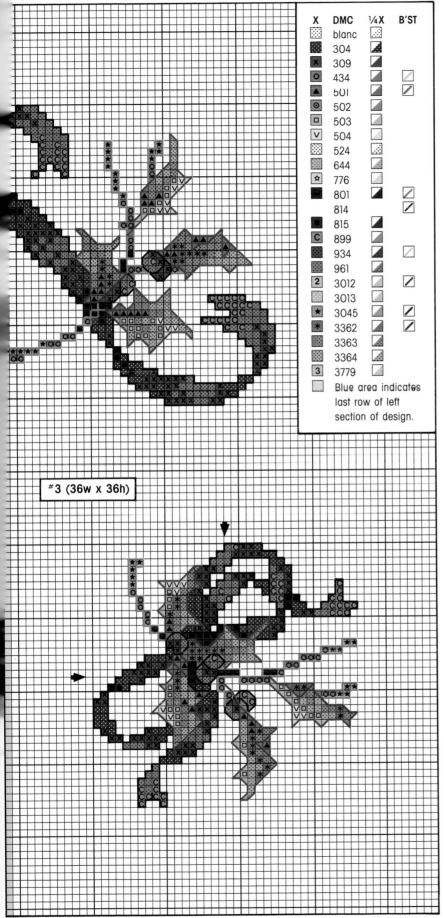

X	DMC	¼X	B'ST
▨	blanc	▨	
▨	304	◪	
✕	309	◪	
⊙	434	◪	◸
▲	501	◪	◸
◉	502	◪	
▢	503	◪	
∨	504	◪	
▨	524	▨	
▨	644	◪	
☆	776	◪	
▨	801	◪	◸
	814		◸
▪	815	◪	
C	899	◪	
▨	934	◪	◸
▨	961	◪	
2	3012	◪	◸
▨	3013	◪	
★	3045	◪	◸
✳	3362	◪	◸
▨	3363	◪	
▨	3364	◪	
3	3779	◪	
▨	Blue area indicates last row of left section of design.		

#3 (36w x 36h)

Holly Table Runner (shown on page 16): Design #1 was stitched over 2 fabric threads across each short end of a 13½" x 44" piece of Cream Bantry Cloth (28 ct). Center design horizontally with bottom of design 2¼" from short edge of fabric. Three strands of floss were used for Cross Stitch and 1 strand for Backstitch. For table runner finishing, see Double Hemstitch Instructions, page 95.

Holly Napkin (shown on page 16): Design #3 was stitched over 2 fabric threads in one corner (refer to photo) of a 13½" square of Cream Bantry Cloth (28 ct) with design 1⅜" from edge of fabric. Three strands of floss were used for Cross Stitch and 1 strand for Backstitch. For napkin finishing, see Double Hemstitch Instructions, page 95.

Holly Sweater (shown on page 16): A portion of Design #1 (refer to photo) was stitched over an 11" x 8" piece of 12 mesh waste canvas on a purchased sweater with top of design ⅝" below bottom of neckband. Three strands of floss were used for Cross Stitch and 1 strand for Backstitch. See Working On Waste Canvas, page 94.

Holly Pillow (shown on page 17): Design #2 was stitched over 2 fabric threads on a 14" x 16" piece of Cream Lugana (25 ct). Three strands of floss were used for Cross Stitch and 1 strand for Backstitch.

For pillow, you will need a 16" x 13¾" piece of fabric for pillow backing, two 4" x 7¾" strips of fabric for side borders, two 4" x 16" strips of fabric for top and bottom borders, 63½" length of ⅜" dia. purchased cording with attached seam allowance, and polyester fiberfill.

Centering design, trim stitched piece to measure 10" x 7¾".

(**Note:** Use ½" seam allowance for all seams.) For pillow front, match right sides and raw edges and sew one side border strip to one short edge of stitched piece. Repeat with remaining side border strip and short edge. Press seam allowances toward strips. Matching right sides and raw edges, sew top border strip to top edge of stitched piece and side strips. Repeat with bottom border strip and bottom edge of stitched piece and side strips. Press seam allowances toward strips.

If needed, trim seam allowance of cording to ½". Start 2" from end of cording; beginning and ending at bottom center of pillow front, baste cording to right side of pillow front making ⅜" clips in seam allowance of cording at each corner. Ends of cording should overlap 4"; turn overlapped ends of cording toward seam allowance and baste across overlapped cording as shown in **Fig. 1**.

Fig. 1

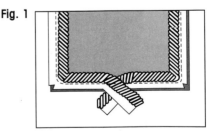

Matching right sides and leaving an opening for turning, use a zipper foot to sew pillow front and backing fabric together. Trim seam allowances diagonally at corners; turn pillow right side out carefully pushing corners outward. Stuff pillow with polyester fiberfill and blind stitch opening closed.

Needlework adaptations by Donna Vermillion Giampa.

55

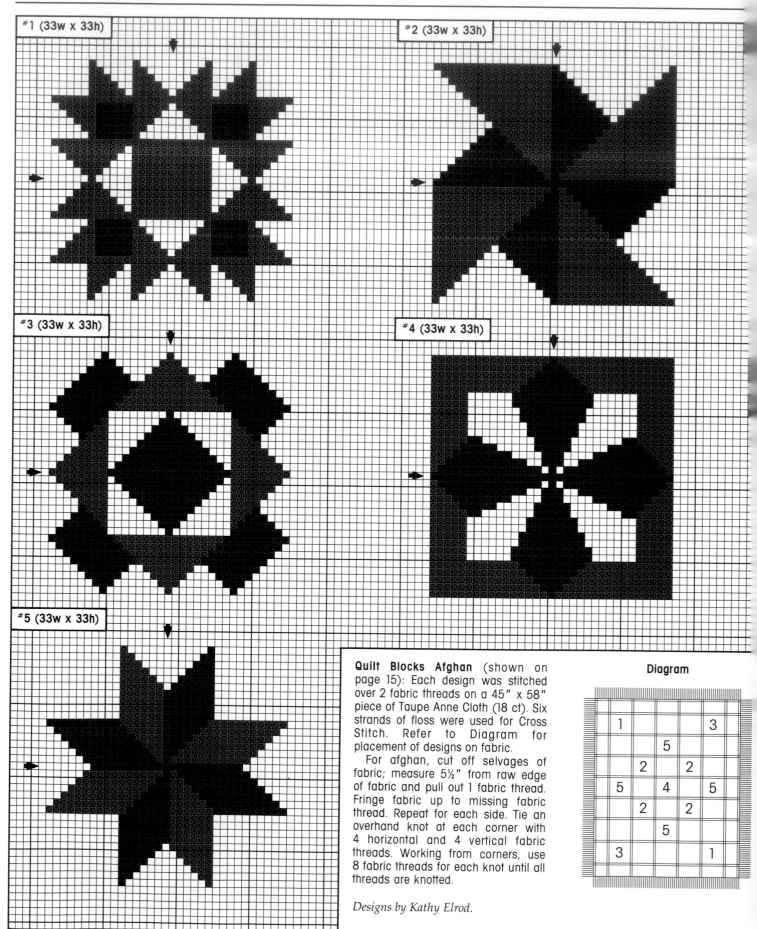

#1 (33w x 33h)

#2 (33w x 33h)

#3 (33w x 33h)

#4 (33w x 33h)

#5 (33w x 33h)

Quilt Blocks Afghan (shown on page 15): Each design was stitched over 2 fabric threads on a 45" x 58" piece of Taupe Anne Cloth (18 ct). Six strands of floss were used for Cross Stitch. Refer to Diagram for placement of designs on fabric.

For afghan, cut off selvages of fabric; measure 5½" from raw edge of fabric and pull out 1 fabric thread. Fringe fabric up to missing fabric thread. Repeat for each side. Tie an overhand knot at each corner with 4 horizontal and 4 vertical fabric threads. Working from corners, use 8 fabric threads for each knot until all threads are knotted.

Designs by Kathy Elrod.

Diagram

1				3
		5		
	2		2	
5		4		5
	2		2	
		5		
3				1

God Bless Our Home in Frame (shown on page 15): The design was stitched on a 9" x 12" sheet of Brown perforated paper (14 ct). Three strands of floss were used for Cross Stitch. It was custom framed.

Design by Linda Culp Calhoun.

Snowflake Scarf (shown on page 10): The design was stitched over a 15" x 8" piece of 14 mesh waste canvas across one short end of a purchased scarf with bottom of design 1" from short edge. Refer to photo for placement of design and repeat to each side. Three strands of floss were used for Cross Stitch. See Working On Waste Canvas, page 94.

Snowflake Sweatshirt (shown on page 12): The design was stitched over a 23" x 10" piece of 8.5 mesh waste canvas on a purchased sweatshirt with set in sleeves. Place top of design 3½" below bottom of neckband with large snowflake centered horizontally; refer to photo and repeat design to each side. Six strands of floss were used for Cross Stitch. See Working On Waste Canvas, page 94.

Snowflake Mittens (shown on page 10): The large snowflake design was stitched over 4" squares of 12 mesh waste canvas on a pair of purchased mittens. Refer to photo for placement of design. Four strands of floss were used for Cross Stitch. See Working On Waste Canvas, page 94.

Snowflake Sweater (shown on page 10): The large and small snowflake designs were worked around the neck of a purchased sweater over 3" squares of 14 mesh waste canvas using Mill Hill Antique Beads-03015. Refer to photo for placement of designs. To attach beads, use 2 strands of floss. See Attaching Beads, page 94 and Working On Waste Canvas, page 94.

Design by Polly Carbonari.

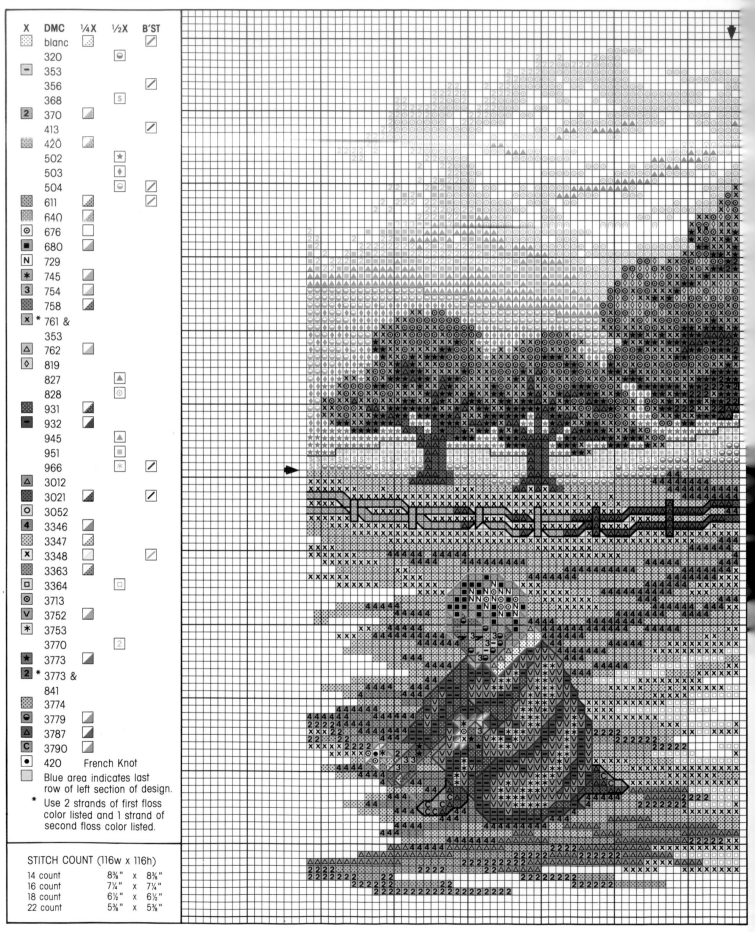

X	DMC	¼X	½X	B'ST
	blanc			
	320		⊝	
−	353			
	356			
	368		S	
2	370			
	413			
	420			
	502		★	
	503		◆	
	504		⊝	
	611			
	640			
⊙	676			
■	680			
N	729			
✶	745			
3	754			
	758			
X	* 761 &			
	353			
△	762			
◇	819			
	827		▲	
	828		⊙	
■	931			
−	932			
	945		▲	
	951		■	
	966		✶	
△	3012			
	3021			
○	3052			
4	3346			
	3347			
X	3348			
	3363			
□	3364		□	
⊙	3713			
V	3752			
✶	3753			
	3770		2	
★	3773			
2	* 3773 &			
	841			
	3774			
⊙	3779			
△	3787			
C	3790			
●	420	French Knot		

Blue area indicates last row of left section of design.

* Use 2 strands of first floss color listed and 1 strand of second floss color listed.

STITCH COUNT (116w x 116h)

14 count	8⅜"	x	8⅜"
16 count	7¼"	x	7¼"
18 count	6½"	x	6½"
22 count	5⅜"	x	5⅜"

Spring Orchard in Frame (shown on page 19): The design was stitched over 2 fabric threads on an 18" square of Antique White Lugana (25 ct). Three strands of floss were used for Cross Stitch and 1 strand for Half Cross Stitch, Backstitch, and French Knot. It was custom framed.

Needlework adaptation by Nancy Dockter.

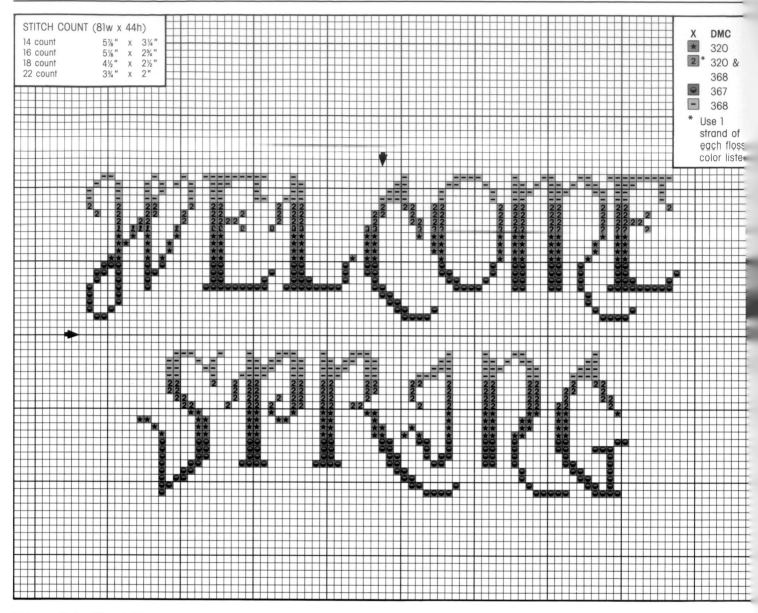

STITCH COUNT (81w x 44h)

14 count	5⅞"	x	3¼"
16 count	5⅛"	x	2¾"
18 count	4½"	x	2½"
22 count	3¾"	x	2"

X	DMC
★	320
2 *	320 & 368
◒	367
-	368

* Use 1 strand of each floss color listed

Welcome Spring Wreath (shown on page 20): The design was stitched over 2 fabric threads on a 13" x 11" piece of Antique White Belfast Linen (32 ct). Two strands of floss were used for Cross Stitch.

For pillow, you will need a 7¾" x 5½" piece of fabric for backing, 3½" x 46" fabric strip for ruffle (pieced as necessary), 2" x 24½" bias fabric strip for cording, 24½" length of ¼" dia. purchased cord, and polyester fiberfill.

Centering design, trim stitched piece to measure 7¾" x 5½".

Center cord on wrong side of bias strip; matching long edges, fold strip over cord. Use a zipper foot to baste along length of strip close to cord; trim seam allowance to ½". Matching raw edges, pin cording to right side of stitched piece, making a ⅜" clip in seam allowance of cording at corners. Ends of cording should overlap approximately 2"; pin overlapping end out of the way. Starting 2" from beginning end of cording and ending 4" from overlapping end, baste cording to stitched piece. On overlapping end of cording, remove 2½" of basting; fold end of fabric back and trim cord so that

it meets beginning end of cord. Fold end of fabric under ½"; wrap fabric over beginning end of cording. Finish basting cording to stitched piece.

For ruffle, press short edges of fabric strip ½" to wrong side. Matching wrong sides and long edges, fold strip in half; press. Machine baste ½" from raw edges, gather fabric strip to fit stitched piece. Matching raw edges, pin ruffle to right side of stitched piece overlapping short ends ¼". Use a ½" seam allowance to sew ruffle to stitched piece.

Matching right sides and leaving an opening for turning, use a ½" seam allowance to sew stitched piece and backing fabric together. Trim seam allowances diagonally at corners; turn pillow right side out carefully pushing corners outward. Stuff pillow with polyester fiberfill and blind stitch opening closed. Attach to a decorated 18" dia. grapevine wreath.

Design by Linda Culp Calhoun.

60

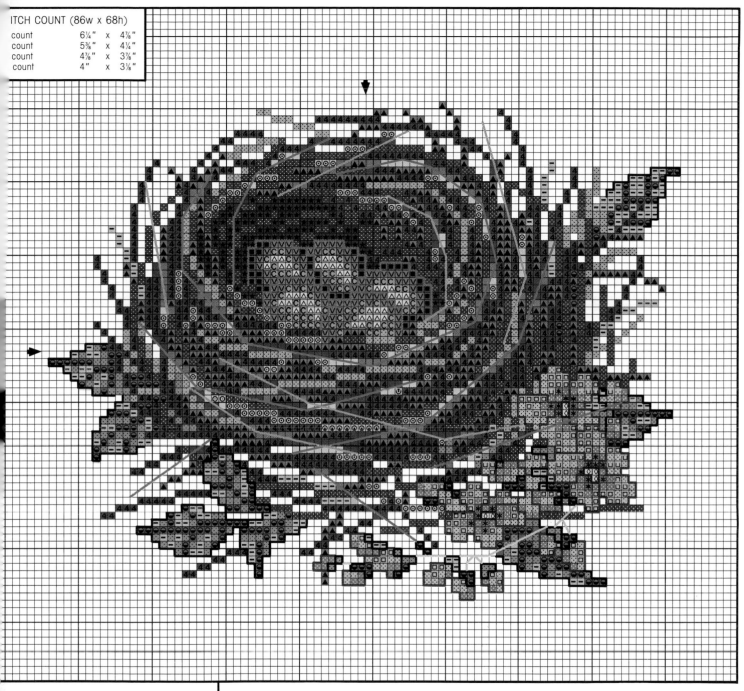

Bird Nest in Frame (shown on page 25): The design was stitched over 2 fabric threads on a 15" x 14" piece of Antique White Lugana (25 ct). Three strands of floss were used for Cross Stitch, 1 strand for Backstitch, and 2 strands for Backstitch worked in long stitches. It was custom framed.

Bird Nest Footstool (shown on page 21): The design was stitched over 2 fabric threads on a 19" x 17" piece of Antique White Aida (18 ct). Six strands of floss were used for Cross Stitch, 2 strands for Backstitch, and 4 strands for Backstitch worked in long stitches. It was mounted on a purchased oval footstool (15" x 11" design area).

Floral Blouse (shown on page 21): A portion of the Bird Nest design (refer to photo) was stitched over 16 mesh waste canvas on the collar of a purchased blouse. Two strands of floss were used for Cross Stitch and 1 strand for Backstitch. See Working On Waste Canvas, page 94.

Needlework adaptation by Jane Chandler.

SPRING

Daffodil Bookmark (shown on page 24): The design was stitched on a 6" x 10" piece of Antique White Aida (14 ct). Three strands of floss were used for Cross Stitch and 1 strand for Backstitch.

For bookmark, you will need a 6" x 10" piece of lightweight cream fabric for backing, hole punch, tracing paper, removable fabric marking pen, fabric stiffener, small foam brush, and a tassel. See Tassel Instructions, page 65.

Apply a heavy coat of fabric stiffener to wrong side of stitched piece using small foam brush. Matching wrong sides, place stitched piece on backing fabric, smoothing stitched piece while pressing fabric pieces together; allow to dry. Apply fabric stiffener to backing fabric; allow to dry. Trace Bookmark Pattern onto tracing paper; cut out pattern. Referring to photo for placement, position pattern on stitched piece. Use fabric marking pen to draw around pattern, remove pattern and cut out along drawn line. Refer to photo and use hole punch to cut hole in end of bookmark.

Place loop of tassel through hole in bookmark; put tassel through loop and pull to tighten.

Daffodil and Iris Sachets (shown on page 24): Each design was stitched over 2 fabric threads on a 9" x 11" piece of Antique White Belfast Linen (32 ct). Two strands of floss were used for Cross Stitch and 1 strand for Backstitch.

For each sachet bag, you will need a 4½" x 7" piece of Belfast Linen for backing, 17" length of 1"w flat lace, 22" length of ¼"w ribbon, polyester fiberfill, and scented oil.

Trim stitched piece to measure 4½" x 7", allowing 1½" margins at sides and bottom of design and a 2⅜" margin at top of design.

Matching right sides and leaving top edge open, use a ½" seam allowance to sew stitched piece and backing fabric together; trim seam allowances diagonally at corners. Turn top edge of bag ¼" to wrong side and press; turn ¼" to wrong side again and hem. Press short edges of lace ½" to wrong side. Machine baste close to straight edge and gather lace to fit top edge of bag. Blind stitch gathered edge of lace to wrong side of top edge of bag. Turn bag right side out and stuff bag with polyester fiberfill. Place a few drops of scented oil on a small amount of fiberfill and insert in middle of bag. Tie ribbon in a bow around bag; trim ends as desired.

Needlework adaptations by Donna Vermillion Giampa.

In the Meadow in Frame (shown on page 22): The design was stitched over 2 fabric threads on a 15" x 18" piece of Antique White Lugana (25 ct). Three strands of floss were used for Cross Stitch and 1 strand for Half Cross Stitch, Backstitch, and French Knot, unless otherwise noted in the color key. It was custom framed.

Needlework adaptation by Sandy Orton of Kooler Design Studio.

X	DMC	¼X	¾X	½X	B'ST	X	DMC	¼X	¾X	½X	B'ST
	blanc			▲			844			■	
⊙	211						898				†
▬	221			◿			926	◿		✕	
⊙	402	◿				*	927 & 598	◿	◿		
	472	◿				▫	928	◿			
	503	◿					935				◿
⊙	504	◿					950	◿		◿	
⫼	550	◿		◿		▫	951	◿			
▣	552	◿				◆	977	◿			
★	553	◿				◇	3013			★	◿ †
	554	◿					3024				
	598			◆			3045	◿			
	610	◿					3046				
△	611						3051				◿ †
	612	◿				3	3052			■	
	632	◿				⊙	3328				◿ †
✱	646	◿		■			3345	◿			
3	647					△	3346	◿			
✚	677	◿					3347	◿			
◆	725	◿				N	3348	◿			
✳	726						3712	◿			
✱	727					◇	3768	◿			
	742	◿				2	3772				
N	743						3773	◿		◿	
▬	744						3776	◿			
■	758	◿	◿				3779	◿			
	760	◿				▢	838	French Knot			
	781			◿							
	783	◿									
■	838	◿		◿							
	* 840 & 3772	◿									
V	* 841 & 3773										

* Use 2 strands of first floss color listed and 1 strand of second floss color listed.

† Use 2 strands of floss for butterfly, mouth, and grass.

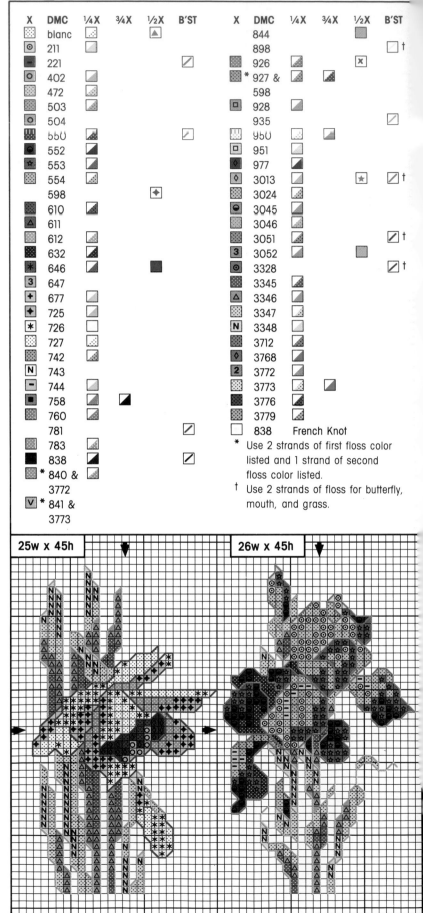

25w x 45h   26w x 45h

STITCH COUNT (87w x 117h)

4 count   6¼" x 8⅜"
6 count   5½" x 7⅜"
8 count   4⅞" x 6½"
2 count   4"   x 5⅜"

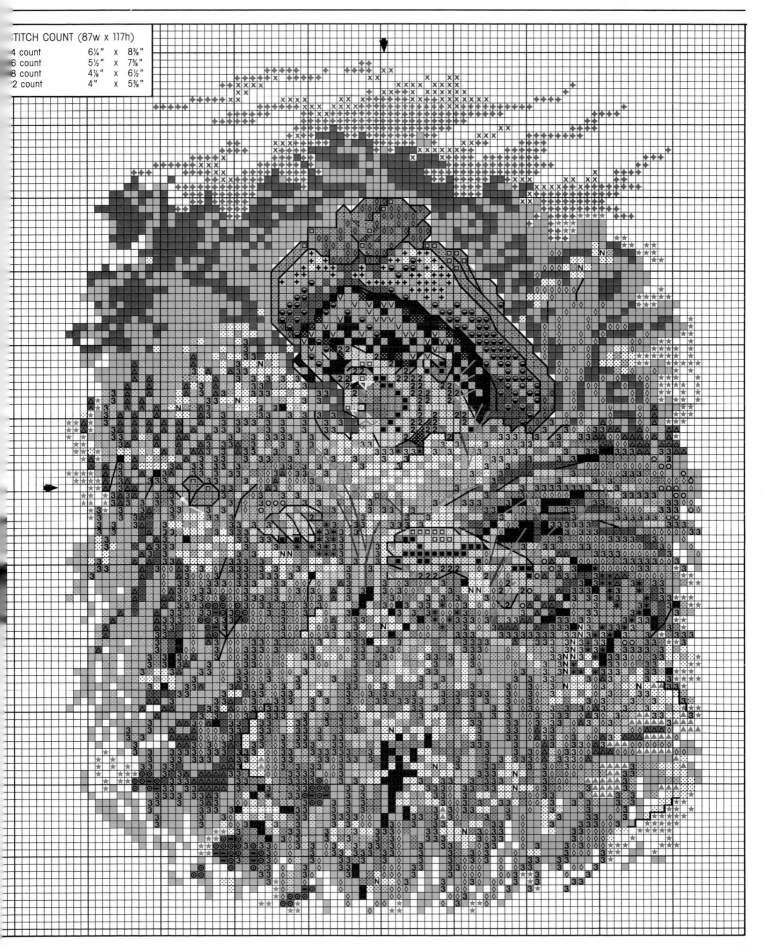

STITCH COUNT (85w x 104h)

count			
14 count	6⅛"	x	7½"
16 count	5⅜"	x	6½"
18 count	4¾"	x	5⅞"
22 count	3⅞"	x	4¾"

center name

A Gift from God to:

center names

Born on this Day:

center date

Needlework adaptation by Nancy Dockter.

X	DMC	¼X	½X	B'ST	X	DMC	¼X	½X	B'ST	X	DMC	¼X	½X	B'ST	X	DMC	¼X	½X	B'ST
	blanc					420					758					869			
	223					422				2	*758 &					948			
	224					610					899					3031			
	317					611					762					3045			
	*353 &					612					813					3046			
	3326					725					826					3047			
	355					744					827					3064			
	356					745					828					3770			
	415					754					831					725	French Knot		
																831	French Knot		

* Use 2 strands of first floss color listed and 1 strand of second floss color listed.

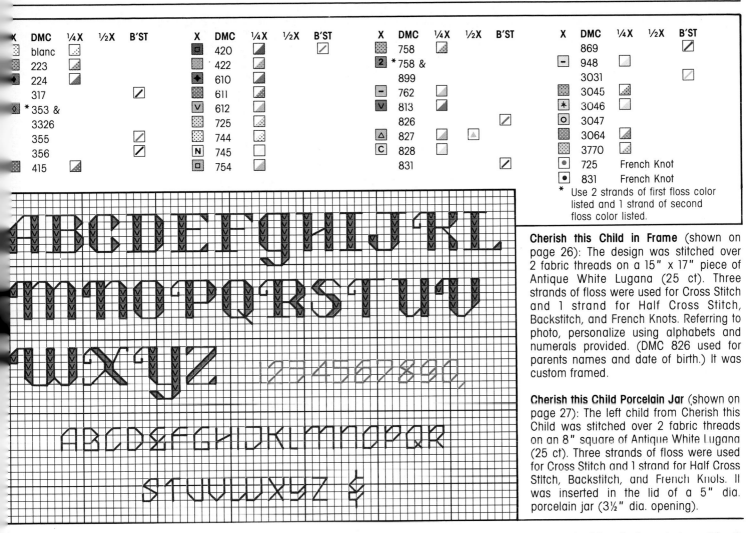

Cherish this Child in Frame (shown on page 26): The design was stitched over 2 fabric threads on a 15" x 17" piece of Antique White Lugana (25 ct). Three strands of floss were used for Cross Stitch and 1 strand for Half Cross Stitch, Backstitch, and French Knots. Referring to photo, personalize using alphabets and numerals provided. (DMC 826 used for parents names and date of birth.) It was custom framed.

Cherish this Child Porcelain Jar (shown on page 27): The left child from Cherish this Child was stitched over 2 fabric threads on an 8" square of Antique White Lugana (25 ct). Three strands of floss were used for Cross Stitch and 1 strand for Half Cross Stitch, Backstitch, and French Knots. It was inserted in the lid of a 5" dia. porcelain jar (3½" dia. opening).

TASSEL INSTRUCTIONS

(shown on page 24, chart on page 62.)

For tassel, you will need one skein of DMC 3364 floss and a 3" square of cardboard. Cut an 8" length of floss to tie end of tassel, cut a 10" length of floss for loop to attach tassel to bookmark, and cut an 18" length of floss to wrap tassel. Wind remainder of floss around the 3" square of cardboard. Insert the 8" length of floss under all strands at one end of cardboard; pull tightly and tie securely; pull knot to inside of tassel and trim ends. To form loop for attaching tassel to bookmark, insert the 10" length of floss under all strands at same end of cardboard; bring ends of length together and tie an overhand knot ½" from ends. Pull knot to inside of tassel. Cut strands at opposite end of cardboard (**Fig. 1**).

To wrap tassel, make a 3" loop at one end of the 18" length of floss; lay loop on tassel as shown in **Fig. 2**. Beginning ¾" from top of tassel and holding loop in place, tightly wrap loose end of length around tassel 6 times (**Fig. 3**).

Place end of length through loop (**Fig 4**). Pull other end of loop, as indicated by arrow in **Fig. 4**, to conceal loop and end of length beneath wrapped area; trim ends.

Evenly trim ends of tassel.

Fig. 2

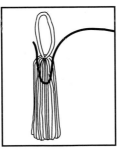

Fig. 4

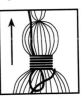

Fig. 1

Fig. 3

SPRING

DESIGN #1
STITCH COUNT (74w x 92h)

count			
14 count	5⅜"	x	6⅝"
16 count	4⅝"	x	5¾"
18 count	4⅛"	x	5⅛"
22 count	3⅜"	x	4¼"

Baby and Bunnies in Frame (shown on page 27): Design #1 was stitched over 2 fabric threads on a 14" x 15" piece of Misty Blue Quaker Cloth (28 ct). Three strands of floss were used for Cross Stitch and 1 strand for Half Cross Stitch and Backstitch.

Needlework adaptation by Sandy Orton of Kooler Design Studio.

X	DMC	¼X	¾X	½X	B'ST		X	DMC	¼X	¾X	½X	B'ST
	blanc						4	3032				
+	ecru						V	3033				
	355							3045				
	434							3064				
5	611						O	3072				*
C	612							3328				
△	646						⊙	★3328 &				
	647							347				
	648			■				3371				
3	676							3712				
-	677							3721				
★	734						x	3722				
	743				*			3753				
◇	758							3773				
2	760							3774				
+	761							3781				
	844				†			3782				
	930						3	3787				
	931						⦿	347	French Knot			
	932							Blue area indicates first row of right section of design.
	950						*	Work in long stitches.
▲	3011						†	Use 844 for Design #1.
	3012							Use 3021 for Design #2.
	3021				†		★	Use 3 strands of each floss color listed.

Apple Blossom Afghan (shown on page 23): Design #2 was stitched over 2 fabric threads on a 45" x 58" piece of Soft White Anne Cloth (18 ct).

For afghan, cut off selvages of fabric; measure 5½" from raw edge of fabric and pull out 1 fabric thread. Fringe fabric up to missing fabric thread. Repeat for each side. Tie an overhand knot at each corner with 4 horizontal and 4 vertical fabric threads. Working from corners, use 8 fabric threads for each knot until all threads are knotted.

Refer to Diagram for placement of design on fabric; use 6 strands of floss for Cross Stitch and 2 strands for Backstitch and French Knots.

Diagram

Needlework adaptation by Nancy Dockter.

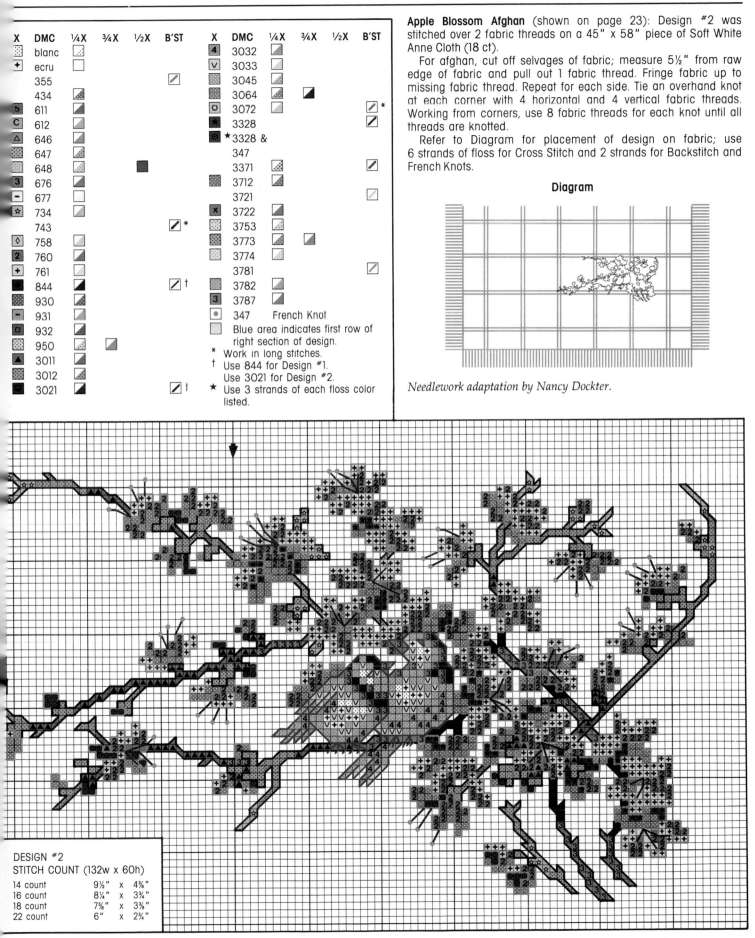

DESIGN #2
STITCH COUNT (132w x 60h)

14 count	9½"	x	4⅜"
16 count	8¼"	x	3¾"
18 count	7⅜"	x	3⅜"
22 count	6"	x	2¾"

SUMMER

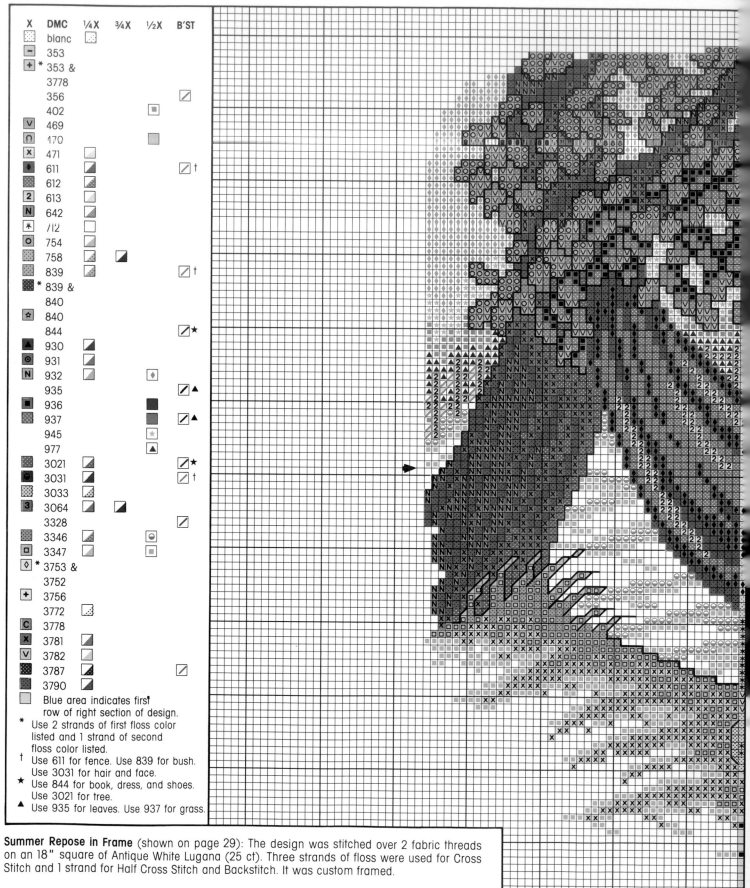

X	DMC	¼X	¾X	½X	B'ST
	blanc				
−	353				
+ *	353 &				
	3778				
	356				◪
	402			▪	
V	469				
∩	470			▪	
X	471	◪			
◆	611	◪			◪ †
	612	◪			
2	613	◪			
N	642	◪			
*	712	◪			
O	754	◪			
	758	◪	◪		
	839	◪			◪ †
*	839 &				
	840				
☆	840				
	844				◪ ★
▲	930	◪			
⊙	931	◪			
N	932	◪		◆	
	935				◪ ▲
■	936			■	
	937			■	◪ ▲
	945			☆	
	977			▲	
	3021	◪			◪ ★
	3031	◪			◪ †
	3033	◪			
3	3064	◪	◪		
	3328				◪
	3346	◪		⊙	
□	3347	◪		■	
◇ *	3753 &				
	3752				
+	3756				
	3772	◪			
C	3778				
X	3781	◪			
V	3782	◪			
	3787	◪			◪
	3790	◪			

☐ Blue area indicates first
   row of right section of design.
* Use 2 strands of first floss color
   listed and 1 strand of second
   floss color listed.
† Use 611 for fence. Use 839 for bush.
   Use 3031 for hair and face.
★ Use 844 for book, dress, and shoes.
   Use 3021 for tree.
▲ Use 935 for leaves. Use 937 for grass.

Summer Repose in Frame (shown on page 29): The design was stitched over 2 fabric threads on an 18" square of Antique White Lugana (25 ct). Three strands of floss were used for Cross Stitch and 1 strand for Half Cross Stitch and Backstitch. It was custom framed.

Needlework adaptation by Nancy Dockter.

STITCH COUNT (116w x 116h)

14 count	8⅜"	x	8⅜"
16 count	7¼"	x	7¼"
18 count	6½"	x	6½"
22 count	5⅜"	x	5⅜"

Clipper Ship in Frame (shown on page 34): The design was stitched over 2 fabric threads on a 20" x 15" piece of Wedgewood Blue Lugana (25 ct). Three strands of floss were used for Cross Stitch, 1 strand of floss or cord for Backstitch, and 1 strand of floss for French Knots, unless otherwise noted in the color key. It was custom framed.

Needlework adaptation by Nancy Dockter.

STITCH COUNT (150w x 89h)		
14 count	10⅜"	x 6⅜"
16 count	9⅜"	x 5⅝"
18 count	8⅜"	x 5"
22 count	6⅞"	x 4"

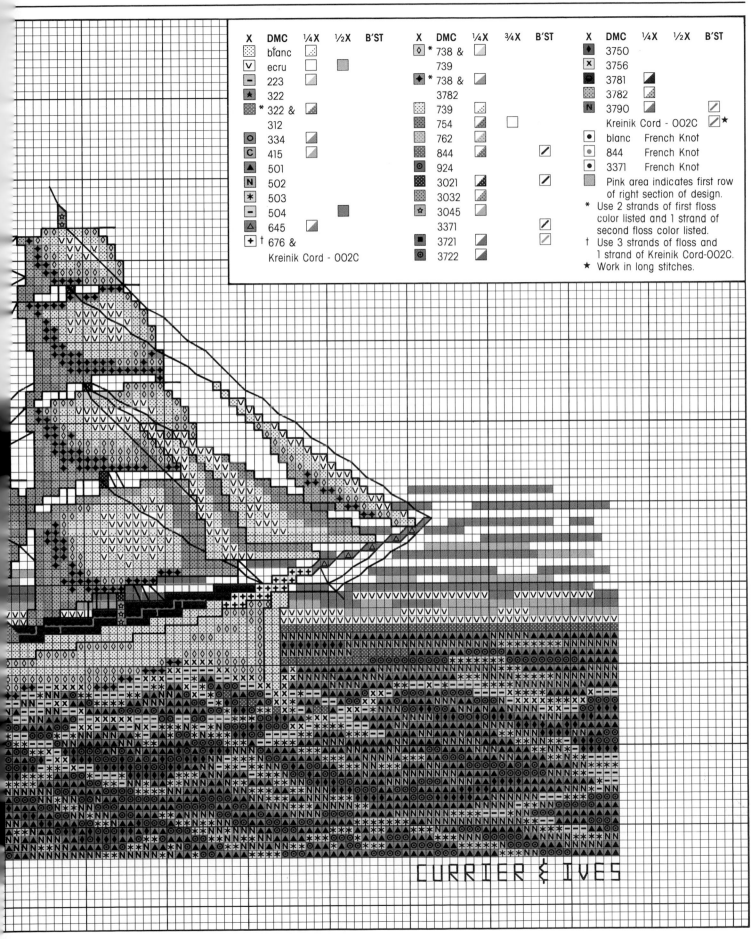

CURRIER & IVES

center names

center date

STITCH COUNT (89w x 121h)

count		
14 count	6⅜"	x 8¾"
16 count	5⅝"	x 7⅝"
18 count	5"	x 6¾"
22 count	4⅛"	x 5½"

Wedding Sampler in Frame (shown on page 36): The design was stitched over 2 fabric threads on a 16" x 18" piece of Ivory Lugana (25 ct). Three strands of floss were used for Cross Stitch and 2 strands for Backstitch. To attach beads, use 1 strand of blanc DMC floss for white beads and 1 strand of 3726 DMC floss for pink beads. See Attaching Beads, page 94. Personalize using alphabet and numerals on page 73. It was custom framed.

Design by Mary Scott.

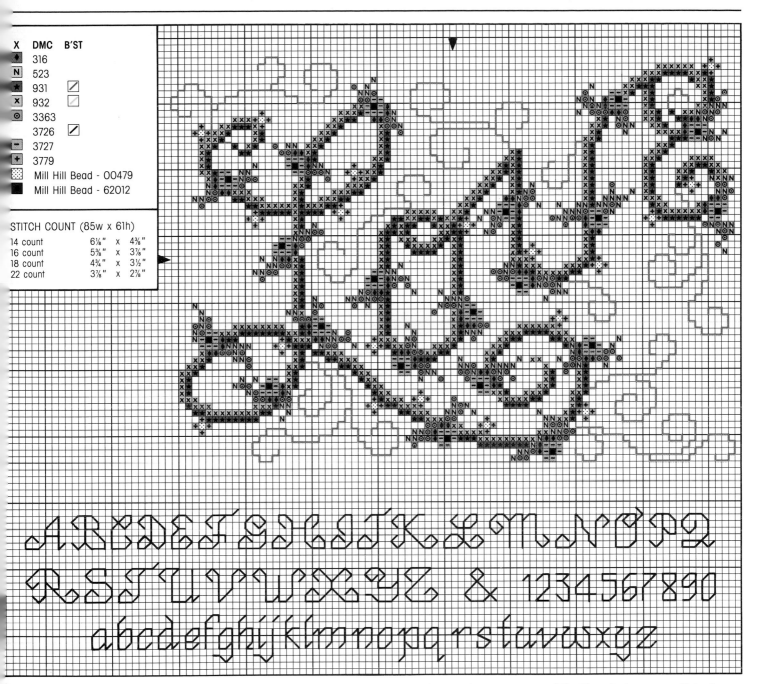

X	DMC	B'ST
◆	316	
N	523	
★	931	◨
X	932	◨
⊙	3363	
	3726	◨
−	3727	
+	3779	
▨	Mill Hill Bead - 00479	
■	Mill Hill Bead - 62012	

STITCH COUNT (85w x 61h)

14 count	6⅛"	x	4⅜"
16 count	5⅜"	x	3⅞"
18 count	4¾"	x	3½"
22 count	3⅞"	x	2⅞"

Sachets (shown on page 37): The heart and "Two Hearts One Love" from Wedding Sampler were each stitched over 2 fabric threads on an 8" square of Ivory Lugana (25 ct). Three strands of floss were used for Cross Stitch and 2 strands for Backstitch. To attach beads, use 1 strand of blanc DMC floss for white beads and 1 strand of 3726 DMC floss for pink beads. See Attaching Beads, page 94.

For heart sachet, you will need a 4" x 3¾" piece of fabric for backing, 1½" x 12½" bias fabric strip for cording, 12½" length of ⅛" dia. purchased cord, polyester fiberfill, and scented oil.

Centering design, trim stitched piece to measure 4" x 3¾". See Heart Sachet Finishing, page 94.

For "Two Hearts One Love" sachet, you will need a 5¼" x 3½" piece of fabric for backing, 1½" x 14½" bias fabric strip for cording, 14½" length of ⅛" dia. purchased cord, 29" length of 1⅜"w flat lace, polyester fiberfill, and scented oil.

Centering design, trim stitched piece to measure 5¼" x 3½". See "Two Hearts One Love" Sachet Finishing, page 94.

Love Pillow (shown on page 37): The design was stitched over 2 fabric threads on a 13" x 15" piece of Ivory Lugana (25 ct). Three strands of floss were used for Cross Stitch and 2 strands for Backstitch. To attach beads, use 1 strand of blanc DMC floss for white beads and 1 strand of 3726 DMC floss for pink beads. See Attaching Beads, page 94.

For pillow, you will need a 10⅜" x 8½" piece of fabric for pillow backing, 2" x 36" bias fabric strip for cording, 36" length of ¼" dia. purchased cord, 35" length of 2¾"w pregathered double lace, and polyester fiberfill.

Centering design, trim stitched piece to measure 10⅜" x 8½". See Love Pillow Finishing, page 94.

Design by Mary Scott.

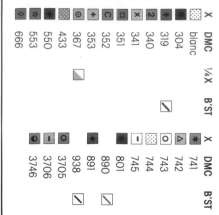

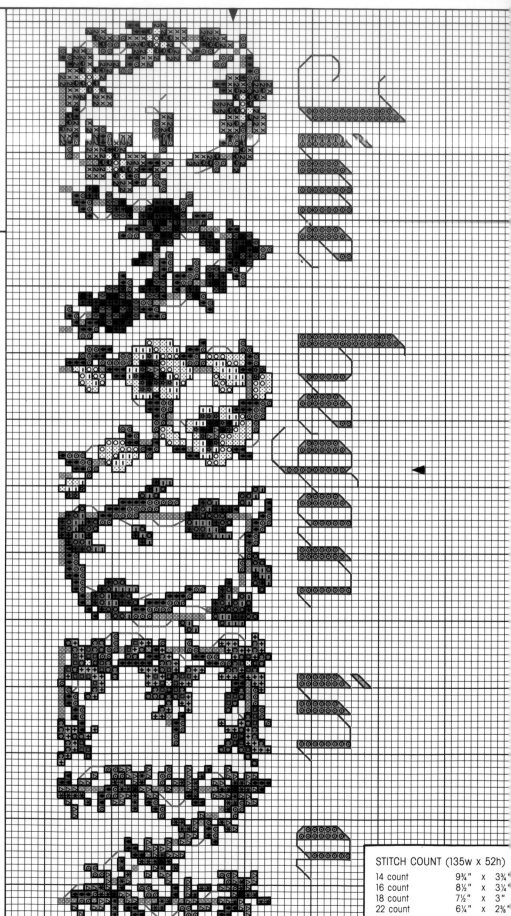

Time Began in a Garden Pillow (shown on page 31): The design was stitched over 2 fabric threads on a 17" x 11" piece of Antique White Belfast Linen (32 ct). Two strands of floss were used for Cross Stitch and 1 strand for Backstitch.

For pillow, you will need a 13" x 7" piece of fabric for backing, 6" x 81" fabric strip for ruffle (pieced as necessary), 2" x 38" bias fabric strip for cording, 38" length of ¼" dia. purchased cord, and polyester fiberfill.

Centering design, trim stitched piece to measure 13" x 7".

Center cord on wrong side of bias strip; matching long edges, fold strip over cord. Use a zipper foot to baste along length of strip close to cord; trim seam allowance to ½". Matching raw edges, pin cording to right side of stitched piece making a ⅜" clip in seam allowance of cording at corners. Ends of cording should overlap approximately 2"; pin overlapping end out of the way. Starting 2" from beginning end of cording and ending 4" from overlapping end, baste cording to stitched piece. On overlapping end of cording, remove 2½" of basting; fold end of fabric back and trim cord so that it meets beginning end of cord. Fold end of fabric under ½"; wrap fabric over beginning end of cording. Finish basting cording to stitched piece.

For ruffle, press short edges of fabric strip ½" to wrong side. Matching wrong sides and long edges, fold strip in half; press. Machine baste ½" from raw edges; gather fabric strip to fit stitched piece. Matching raw edges, pin ruffle to right side of stitched piece overlapping short ends ¼". Use a ½" seam allowance to sew ruffle to stitched piece.

Matching right sides and leaving an opening for turning, use a ½" seam allowance to sew stitched piece and backing fabric together. Trim seam allowances diagonally at corners; turn pillow right side out carefully pushing corners outward. Stuff pillow with polyester fiberfill and blind stitch opening closed.

Design by Jane Chandler.

STITCH COUNT (135w x 52h)		
14 count	9¾"	x 3¾"
16 count	8½"	x 3¼"
18 count	7½"	x 3"
22 count	6¼"	x 2⅜"

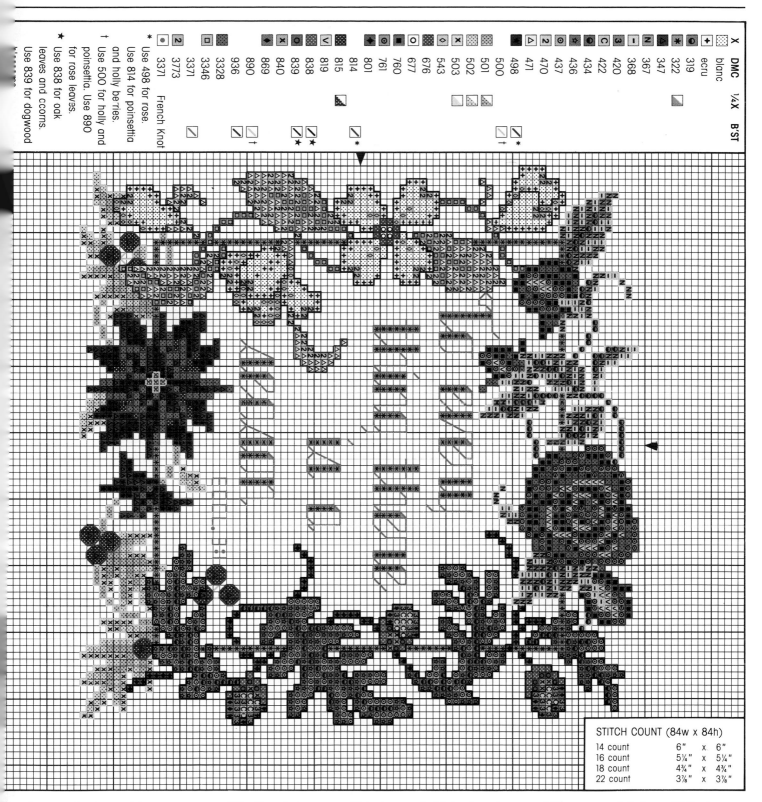

X	DMC	1/4X	B'ST
	blanc		
	ecru		
	319		
	322		
	347		
	367		
	368		
	420		
	422		
	434		
	436		
	437		
	470		
	471		
	498		
	500		
	501		
	502		
	503		
	543		
	676		
	677		
	760		
	761		
	801		
	814		
	815		
	819		
	838		
	839		
	840		
	869		
	890		
	936		
	3328		
	3346		
	3371		
	3373		
	3371		

★ French Knot 3371

* Use 498 for rose.
Use 814 for poinsettia and holly berries.
† Use 500 for holly and poinsettia. Use 890 for rose leaves.
★ Use 838 for oak leaves and acorns. Use 839 for dogwood...

STITCH COUNT (84w x 84h)

14 count	6"	x 6"
16 count	5¼"	x 5¼"
18 count	4¾"	x 4¾"
22 count	3⅞"	x 3⅞"

Four Seasons in Frame (shown on page 30): The design was stitched over 2 fabric threads on a 15" square of Antique White Lugana (25 ct). Three strands of floss were used for Cross Stitch and 1 strand for Backstitch and French Knots. It was custom framed.

Seasonal Bookmarks (shown on page 31): The dogwood and roses from Four Seasons (refer to photo) were each stitched on a 6" x 12" piece of Antique White Belfast Linen (32 ct). Two strands of floss were used for Cross Stitch and 1 strand for Backstitch.
Centering design, trim stitched piece to measure 3" x 9". On one short edge, measure 1½" from raw edge of fabric and pull out 1 fabric thread. Fringe fabric up to missing fabric thread, repeat for remaining short edge. On one long edge, turn fabric ¼" to wrong side and press; turn ¼" to wrong side again and hem. Repeat for remaining long edge.

Design by Jane Chandler.

STITCH COUNT (112w x 109h)		
14 count	8"	x 7⅞"
16 count	7"	x 6⅞"
18 count	6¼"	x 6⅛"
22 count	5⅛"	x 5"

Sea Fever

I must down to the seas again
to the lonely sea and the sky,
And all I ask is a tall ship
and a star to steer her by,
And the wheel's kick
and the wind's song
and the white sail's shaking,
And a grey mist
on the sea's face
and a grey dawn breaking.
I must down to the seas again
for the call of the running tide
Is a wild call and a clear call
that may not be denied.

John Masefield

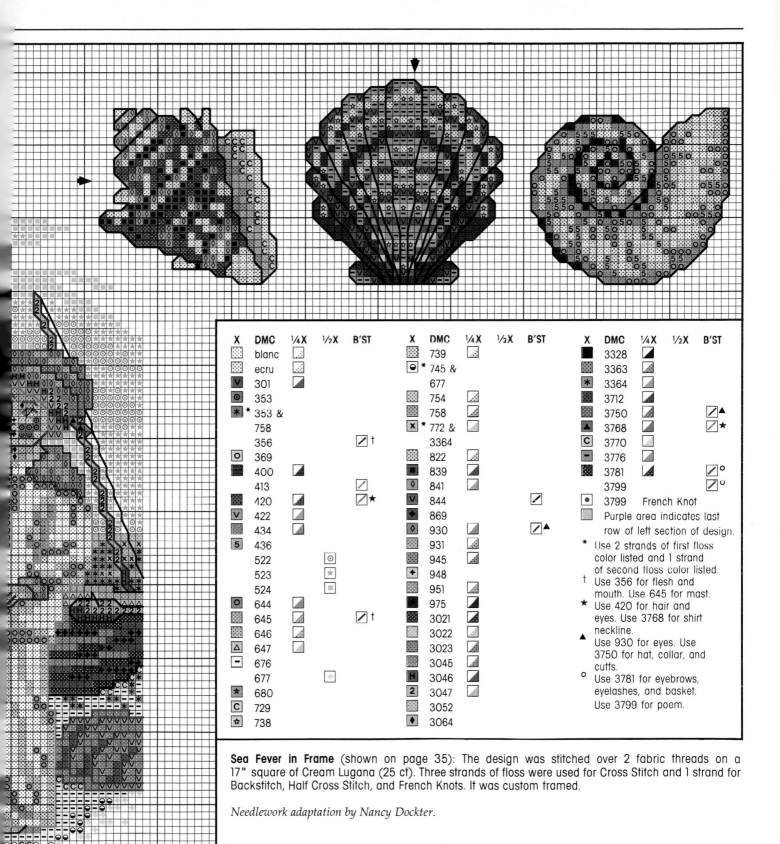

X	DMC	¼X	½X	B'ST		X	DMC	¼X	½X	B'ST		X	DMC	¼X	½X	B'ST
	blanc						739						3328			
	ecru					⊖	* 745 &						3363			
V	301						677					*	3364			
⊙	353						754						3712			
*	* 353 &						758						3750			▲
	758					X	* 772 &					▲	3768			★
	356			▢ †			3364					C	3770			
⊙	369						822					-	3776			
	400						839						3781			°
	413					◇	841						3799			°
	420			★		V	844					•	3799	French Knot		
V	422						869						Purple area indicates last			
	434					◇	930			▲			row of left section of design.			
5	436						931									
	522						945						* Use 2 strands of first floss			
	523					✦	948						color listed and 1 strand			
	524						951						of second floss color listed.			
⊙	644						975						† Use 356 for flesh and			
	645			†			3021						mouth. Use 645 for mast.			
	646						3022						★ Use 420 for hair and			
△	647						3023						eyes. Use 3768 for shirt			
-	676						3045						neckline.			
	677					H	3046						▲ Use 930 for eyes. Use			
★	680					2	3047						3750 for hat, collar, and			
C	729						3052						cuffs.			
☆	738					◆	3064						° Use 3781 for eyebrows,			
													eyelashes, and basket.			
													Use 3799 for poem.			

Sea Fever in Frame (shown on page 35): The design was stitched over 2 fabric threads on a 17" square of Cream Lugana (25 ct). Three strands of floss were used for Cross Stitch and 1 strand for Backstitch, Half Cross Stitch, and French Knots. It was custom framed.

Needlework adaptation by Nancy Dockter.

Seaside Collection in Frame (shown on page 35): The designs were stitched on a 10" x 14" piece of Natural Aida (16 ct) aligning the bottom of the designs and leaving 8 spaces between each shell. Two strands of floss were used for Cross Stitch and 1 strand for Backstitch. It was custom framed.

Designs by Jane Chandler.

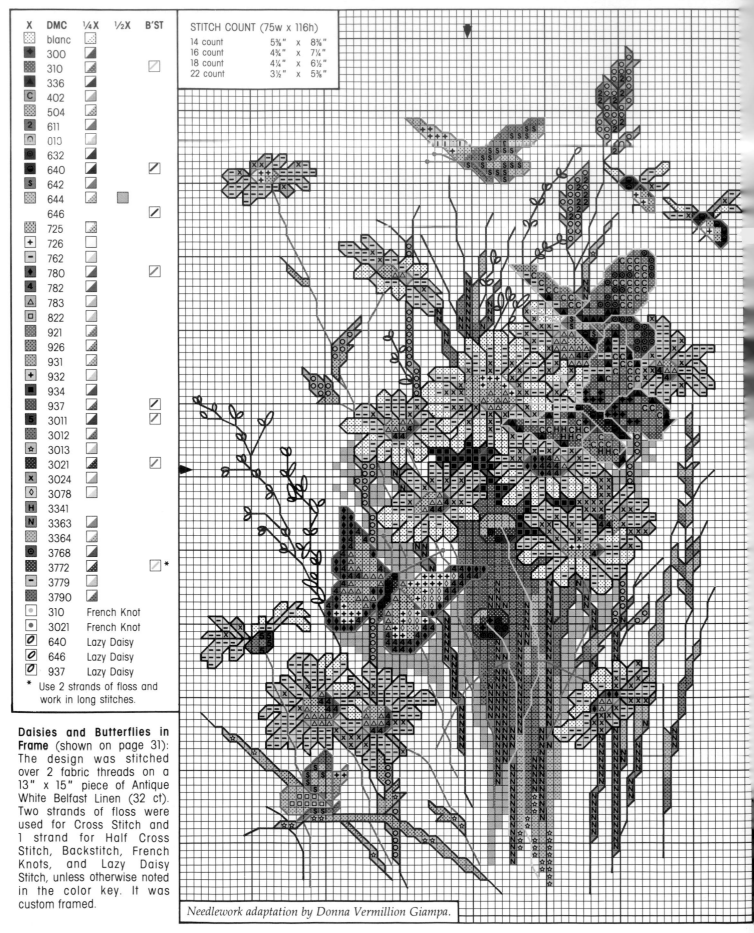

X	DMC	1/4X	1/2X	B'ST
	blanc			
	300			
	310			✓
	336			
C	402			
	504			
2	611			
∩	010			
	632			
	640			✓
S	642			
	644		▨	
	646			✓
	725			
+	726			
-	762			
♦	780			✓
4	782			
△	783			
□	822			
	921			
	926			
	931			
+	932			
■	934			
	937			✓
5	3011			✓
	3012			
☆	3013			
	3021			✓
×	3024			
◇	3078			
H	3341			
N	3363			
	3364			
◎	3768			
	3772			✓ *
-	3779			
	3790			
◦	310	French Knot		
●	3021	French Knot		
∅	640	Lazy Daisy		
∅	646	Lazy Daisy		
∅	937	Lazy Daisy		

* Use 2 strands of floss and work in long stitches.

STITCH COUNT (75w x 116h)

14 count	5⅜"	x	8⅜"
16 count	4¾"	x	7¼"
18 count	4¼"	x	6½"
22 count	3½"	x	5⅜"

Daisies and Butterflies in Frame (shown on page 31): The design was stitched over 2 fabric threads on a 13" x 15" piece of Antique White Belfast Linen (32 ct). Two strands of floss were used for Cross Stitch and 1 strand for Half Cross Stitch, Backstitch, French Knots, and Lazy Daisy Stitch, unless otherwise noted in the color key. It was custom framed.

Needlework adaptation by Donna Vermillion Giampa.

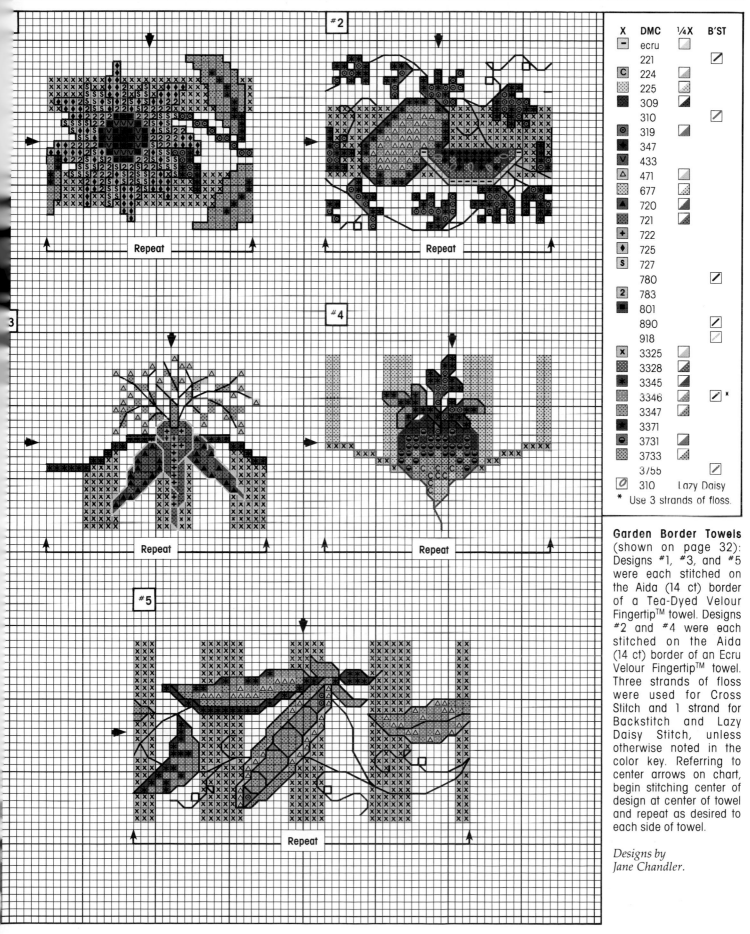

Garden Border Towels
(shown on page 32):
Designs #1, #3, and #5
were each stitched on
the Aida (14 ct) border
of a Tea-Dyed Velour
Fingertip™ towel. Designs
#2 and #4 were each
stitched on the Aida
(14 ct) border of an Ecru
Velour Fingertip™ towel.
Three strands of floss
were used for Cross
Stitch and 1 strand for
Backstitch and Lazy
Daisy Stitch, unless
otherwise noted in the
color key. Referring to
center arrows on chart,
begin stitching center of
design at center of towel
and repeat as desired to
each side of towel.

Designs by
Jane Chandler.

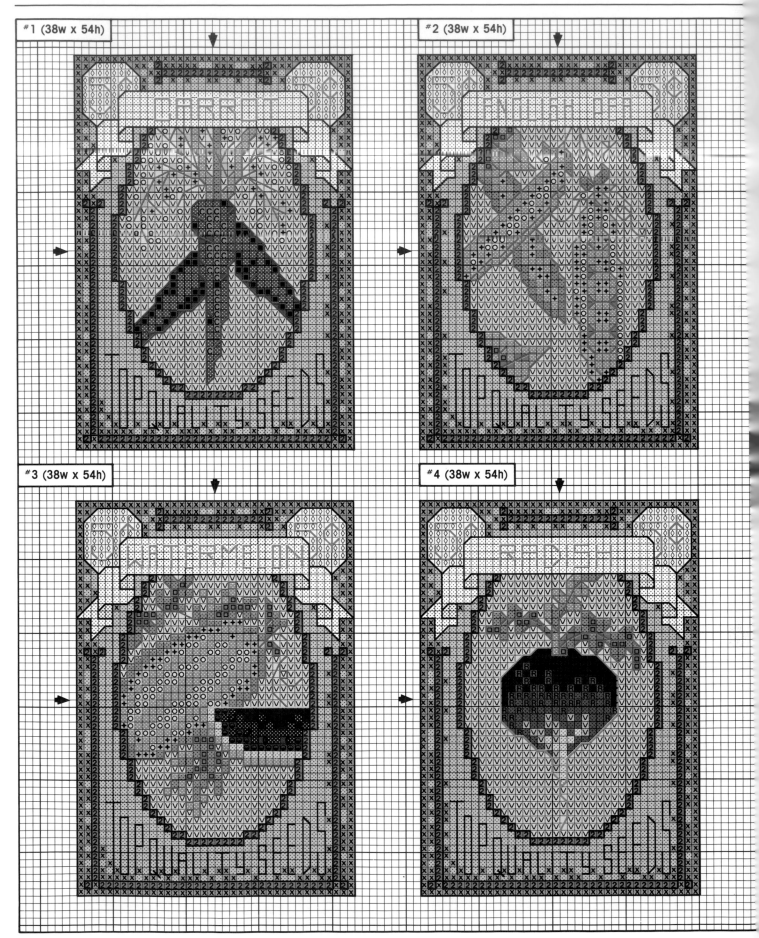

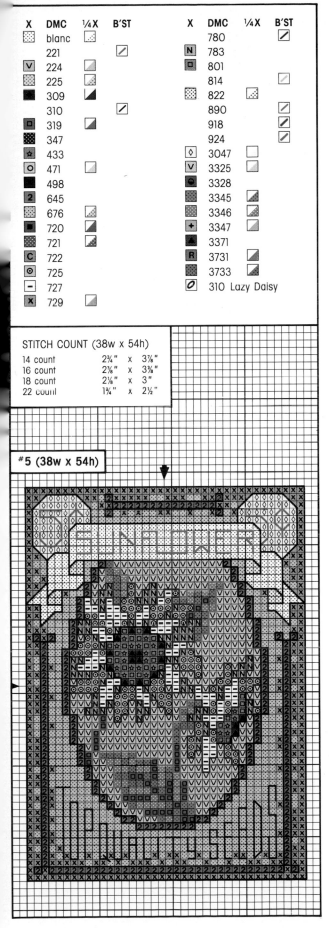

X	DMC	1/4X	B'ST	X	DMC	1/4X	B'ST
▨	blanc	▨			780		/
	221		/	N	783		
V	224	/	/	□	801		
▨	225	/			814		/
■	309	◣		▨	822	▨	
	310		/		890		/
□	319	/			918		/
▨	347				924		/
★	433	□		◇	3047	□	
O	471	/		V	3325	/	
■	498			◉	3328	/	
2	645			▨	3345	◣	
▨	676	▨		▨	3346	◣	
■	720	/		+	3347	/	
▨	721	▨		▲	3371		
C	722	▨		R	3731	◣	
◉	725			▨	3733	◣	
-	727			O	310 Lazy Daisy		
X	729	/					

STITCH COUNT (38w x 54h)

14 count	2¾"	x 3⅞"
16 count	2⅜"	x 3⅜"
18 count	2⅛"	x 3"
22 count	1¾"	x 2½"

#5 (38w x 54h)

Seed Packet Plant Pokes (shown on page 32): Each design was stitched on an 8" x 9" piece of Natural Aida (16 ct). Two strands of floss were used for Cross Stitch and 1 strand for Backstitch and Lazy Daisy Stitch.

For each plant poke, you will need an 8" x 9" piece of lightweight cream fabric for backing, craft stick, clear-drying craft glue, fabric stiffener, and small foam brush.

Apply a heavy coat of fabric stiffener to wrong side of stitched piece using small foam brush. Matching wrong sides, place stitched piece on backing fabric, smoothing stitched piece while pressing fabric pieces together; allow to dry. Apply fabric stiffener to backing fabric; allow to dry. Cut out close to edges of stitched design. Refer to photo to glue craft stick to back of each stitched piece.

Seed Packet Shirt (shown on page 33): Design #1 (omitting blue background) was stitched over an 8" square of 14 mesh waste canvas on the pocket of a purchased chambray shirt with top of design approximately ⅜" below top edge of pocket. Three strands of floss were used for Cross Stitch and 1 strand for Backstitch. See Working On Waste Canvas, page 94.

Seed Packet Pillows (shown on page 33): Designs #3 and #5 were each stitched over 2 fabric threads on a 13" x 14" piece of New Khaki Davosa (18 ct). Five strands of floss were used for Cross Stitch and 2 strands for Backstitch and Lazy Daisy Stitch.

For each pillow, you will need a 6½" x 11" piece of lightweight fabric for lining stitched piece, two 14" x 11" pieces of fabric for pillow front and backing, 2" x 22" bias fabric strip for ¼" dia. cord, 22" length of ¼" dia. purchased cord, 2½" x 50" bias fabric strip for ⅜" dia. cord, 50" length of ⅜" dia. purchased cord, and polyester fiberfill.

Centering design, trim stitched piece to measure 6½" x 11"; baste lining fabric to wrong side of stitched piece close to raw edges.

Center ¼" dia. cord on wrong side of bias strip; matching long edges, fold strip over cord. Use a zipper foot to baste along length of strip close to cord; trim seam allowance to ½" and cut length of cording in half. Matching raw edges, baste one length of cording to right side of one long edge of stitched piece. Press seam allowance toward stitched piece. Repeat with remaining length of cording and long edge of stitched piece.

For pillow front, center wrong side of stitched piece on right side of one 14" x 11" piece of fabric; baste in place. Using zipper foot and same color thread as cording, attach stitched piece to pillow front by sewing through all layers as close as possible to cording, taking care not to catch fabric of stitched piece.

Center ⅜" dia. cord on wrong side of bias strip; matching long edges, fold strip over cord. Baste along length of strip close to cord; trim seam allowance to ½". Matching raw edges, pin cording to right side of pillow front, making a ⅜" clip in seam allowance of cording at corners. Ends of cording should overlap approximately 2"; pin overlapping end out of the way. Starting 2" from beginning end of cording and ending 4" from overlapping end, baste cording to pillow front. On overlapping end of cording, remove 2½" of basting; fold end of fabric back and trim cord so that it meets beginning end of cord. Fold end of fabric under ½"; wrap fabric over beginning end of cording. Finish basting cording to pillow front.

Matching right sides and leaving an opening for turning, use a ½" seam allowance to sew pillow front and backing fabric together. Trim seam allowances diagonally at corners; turn pillow right side out carefully pushing corners outward. Stuff pillow with polyester fiberfill; blind stitch opening closed.

Designs by Jane Chandler.

X	DMC	¼X	½X	B'ST
▨	221	◢		
−	223	◢		
○	224			
	317		★	
▢	318	◢	◉	
C	353			
4	355	◢		
V	356	◢		
☆	402	◢	△	
▨	407	◢		
◆	413	◢		◢
▨	414	◢	×	
⊖	420	◢		
░	422	◢		
◐	451	◢		
✳	452	◢		
░	453	◢		
★	610	◢		
	611			◢
▨	612	◢		
◆	632	◢	■	
S	676	◢		
	722		✳	
▨	729	◢		
×	738	◢		
◇	762	◢		
	839			◢
■	869	◢		◢
▨	918	◢		
✳	920	◢		
C	921	◢		
▨	922	◢		
▨	930	◢		◢
◉	931	◢		
◆	932	◢		
	945		✚	
☆	950	◢		
▲	3011	◢	◆	◢
2	3012	◢	◉	
O	3013	◢	◈	
▨	3045	◢		
△	3064	◢	4	
▨	3328	◢		◢
▨	3721	◢		
▢	3722	◢		
░	3770	░		
N	3772	◢	V	
░	3774	░		
■	3777	◢		
5	3778			
	3787			◢

▨ Blue area indicates first row of right section of design.

Autumn Harvest in Frame (shown on page 39): The design was stitched over 2 fabric threads on an 18" square of Antique White Lugana (25 ct). Three strands of floss were used for Cross Stitch and 1 strand for Half Cross Stitch and Backstitch. It was custom framed.

Needlework adaptation by Nancy Dockter.

STITCH COUNT (116w x 116h)

14 count	8⅜"	x	8⅜"
16 count	7¼"	x	7¼"
18 count	6½"	x	6½"
22 count	5⅜"	x	5⅜"

AUTUMN

X	DMC	¼X	½X	B'ST
-	ecru			
	225			
△	317			
	319			
	367			
△	368			
V	369			
	371			
	372			
*	402 & 977			
2	435			
*	436 & 922			
+	451			
▲	500			
	520			
☆	610			
	611			
4 *	676 & 402			
3	760			
S	761			
	840			
	921			
⊙	922			
*	930 & 413			
-	931			
	932			
✳	935			
△	948			
◇	951			
	987			
+	3011			
4	3012			
R	3031			
H	3045			
O	3046			
	3051			
	3347			
⊙	3348			
5	3362			
C	3363			
☆	3364			
	3371			
	3712			
x	3753			
	3781			
⚜	3799			
2 *	3799 & 3750			

STITCH COUNT (146w x 102h)

14 count	10½" x	7⅜"
16 count	9⅛" x	6⅜"
18 count	8⅛" x	5¾"
22 count	6¾" x	4¾"

Pink area indicates first row of right section of design.

* Use 2 strands of first floss color listed and 1 strand of second floss color listed.

Bountiful Harvest in Frame
(shown on page 40): The design was stitched over 2 fabric threads on a 19" x 16" piece of Platinum Cashel Linen (28 ct). Three strands of floss were used for Cross Stitch and 1 strand for Half Cross Stitch and Backstitch. It was custom framed.

Needlework adaptation by Nancy Dockter.

CURRIER & IVES

X	DMC	1/4X	B'ST	X	DMC	1/4X	B'ST
○	223			★	936		
-	224			S	3041		
✕	327			3	3346		
▲	400			◆	3721		
V	402			△	3722		
N	420			◉	3776		
◉	* 501 & 500				Blue area indicates first row of right section of design.		
△	502						
☆	676				* For framed piece, use 1 strand of each floss color listed. For tray, use 2 strands of first floss color listed and 1 strand of second floss color listed.		
◆	729						
■	733						
	792	◪					
◉	* 792 & 796						
◉	793	◪					
+	809						
✳	898						
■	902	◪					

Fruit Basket Sampler in Frame (shown on page 45): The design was stitched over 2 fabric threads on a 17" x 15" piece of Raw Belfast Linen (32 ct). Two strands of floss were used for Cross Stitch and Backstitch. Date sampler using numerals provided. It was custom framed.

Fruit Basket Tray (shown on page 44): The basket of fruit from the Fruit Basket Sampler was stitched over 2 fabric threads on a 13" x 10" piece of Raw Dublin Linen (25 ct). Three strands of floss were used for Cross Stitch. It was inserted in a purchased tray (12" x 9" opening; custom mat with 9" x 6" oval opening).

Design by Sandy Orton of Kooler Design Studio.

STITCH COUNT (140w x 110h)

count			
14 count	10"	x	7⅞"
16 count	8¾"	x	6⅞"
18 count	7⅞"	x	6⅛"
22 count	6⅜"	x	5"

center year

AUTUMN

X	DMC	¼X	B'ST
	blanc		
	223		
	353		
	367		
C	407		
	434		
	646		
J	648		
	676		
	733		
	734		
	754		
	758		
4	760		
	801		
2	813		
	826		
	827		
	902		
	938		∕
V	948		
	976		
O	989		
S	3045		
	3046		
+	3047		
	3328		
5	3721		

STITCH COUNT (28w x 112h)

14 count	2"	x	8"
16 count	1¾"	x	7"
18 count	1⅝"	x	6¼"
22 count	1⅜"	x	5⅛"

Autumn Children Bookmarks (shown on page 47): Each design was stitched on an Ecru Stitch-N-Mark™ bookmark (18 ct). Two strands of floss were used for Cross Stitch and 1 strand for Backstitch.

Needlework adaptation by Sandy Orton of Kooler Design Studio.

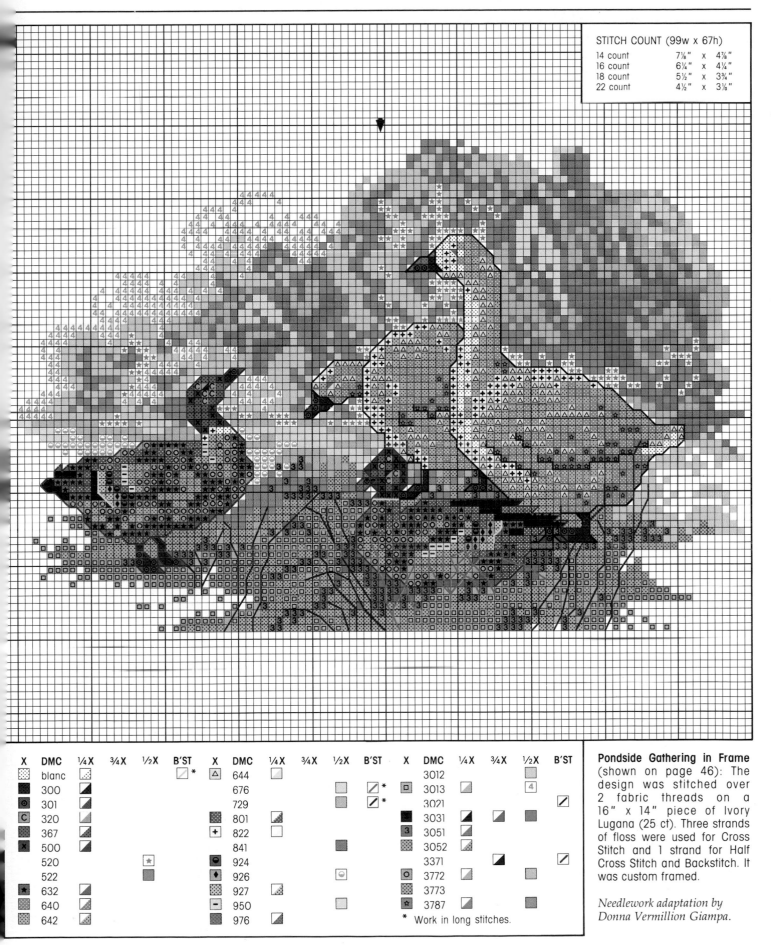

STITCH COUNT (99w x 67h)		
14 count	7⅛"	x 4⅞"
16 count	6¼"	x 4¼"
18 count	5½"	x 3¾"
22 count	4½"	x 3⅛"

X	DMC	¼X	¾X	½X	B'ST	X	DMC	¼X	¾X	½X	B'ST	X	DMC	¼X	¾X	½X	B'ST
	blanc				*	△	644						3012				
	300						676				*		3013				
⊙	301						729				*		3021				
C	320						801						3031				
	367					+	822					3	3051				
✕	500						841						3052				
	520		★			⊖	924						3371				
	522					◆	926					○	3772				
★	632						927						3773				
	640					−	950					✿	3787				
	642						976										

* Work in long stitches.

Pondside Gathering in Frame (shown on page 46): The design was stitched over 2 fabric threads on a 16" x 14" piece of Ivory Lugana (25 ct). Three strands of floss were used for Cross Stitch and 1 strand for Half Cross Stitch and Backstitch. It was custom framed.

Needlework adaptation by Donna Vermillion Giampa.

AUTUMN

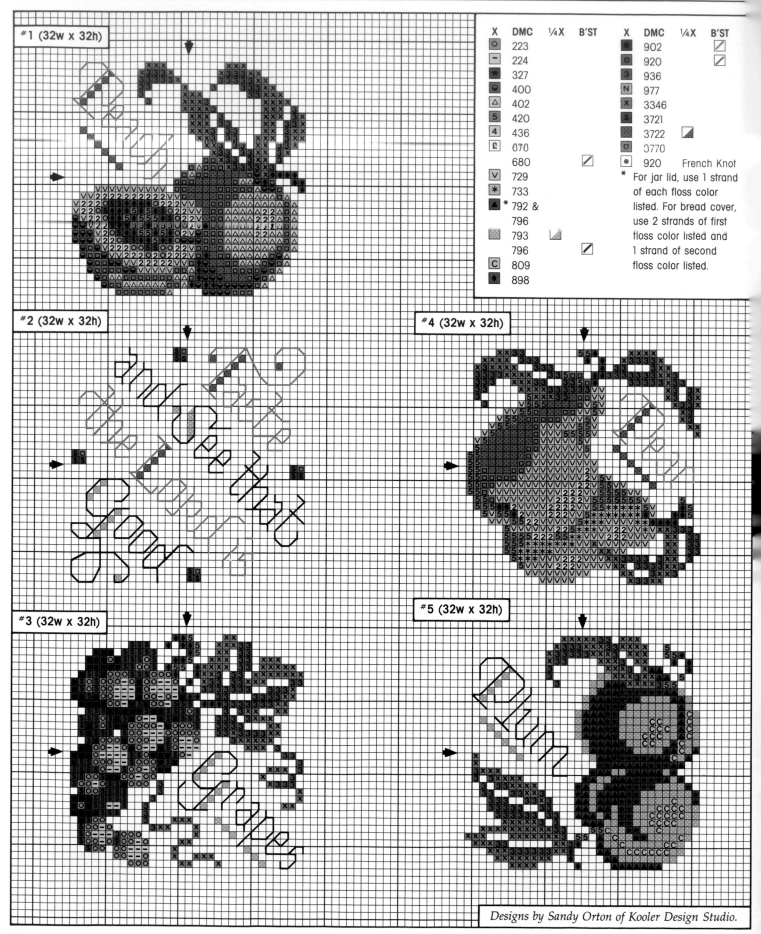

#1 (32w x 32h)

#2 (32w x 32h)

#3 (32w x 32h)

#4 (32w x 32h)

#5 (32w x 32h)

X	DMC	1/4X	B'ST		X	DMC	1/4X	B'ST
O	223				■	902		/
−	224				◉	920		/
★	327				3	936		
☻	400				N	977		
△	402				X	3346		
5	420				S	3721		
4	436				▨	3722	/	
ℒ	070				▢	0770		
	680		/		●	920	French Knot
V	729							
*	733							
▲	*792 &							
	796							
▨	793	◢						
	796		/					
C	809							
◆	898							

* For jar lid, use 1 strand of each floss color listed. For bread cover, use 2 strands of first floss color listed and 1 strand of second floss color listed.

Designs by Sandy Orton of Kooler Design Studio.

Design by Linda Culp Calhoun.

Harvest Bread Covers (shown on page 42): Designs #1, #3, and #5 were each stitched on one corner of a Country Oatmeal Royal Classic™ Breadcover (14 ct) with design 7 fabric threads from beginning of fringe. Three strands of floss were used for Cross Stitch and 2 strands for Backstitch.

Harvest Skirted Jar Lids (shown on page 43): Designs #1, #3, and #5 were each stitched on an 8" square of Natural Aida (16 ct). Two strands of floss were used for Cross Stitch and 1 strand for Backstitch.

For each skirted jar lid, you will need a wide mouth jar lid, 7½" square of fabric, 3¼" dia. circle of adhesive mounting board, 3¼" dia. circle of batting, 18" length of raffia, rubber band, and clear-drying craft glue.

Centering design, trim stitched piece to a 6½" square; fringe edges of stitched piece ¼" on all sides. If desired, use pinking shears and trim all sides of fabric square.

Remove paper from adhesive mounting board; center batting on adhesive board and press in place. With batting facing up, glue board inside jar lid.

Center wrong side of stitched piece on right side of fabric square; center on jar lid and place rubber band around lid to hold in place. Refer to photo to tie raffia over rubber band around jar lid.

Harvest Jar Lids (shown on page 43): Designs #2 and #4 were each stitched on an 8" square of Natural Aida (16 ct). Two strands of floss were used for Cross Stitch and 1 strand for Backstitch.

For each jar lid, you will need a wide mouth jar lid, 3¼" dia. circle of adhesive mounting board, 3¼" dia. circle of batting, 1" x 25" torn fabric strip for trim, and clear-drying craft glue.

Centering design, trim stitched piece to a 5¼" dia. circle.

Remove paper from adhesive mounting board; center batting on adhesive board and press in place. With right side facing up, center stitched piece on batting. Fold edges of stitched piece to back of adhesive board; glue fabric edges to back of adhesive board. Glue

stitched piece inside jar lid. Refer to photo to tie fabric strip around jar lid edge.

"He Crowneth the Year" Pillow (shown on page 47): The design was stitched over 2 fabric threads on an 11" x 9" piece of Cream Belfast Linen (32 ct). Two strands of floss were used for Cross Stitch and 1 strand for Backstitch and French Knots.

For pillow, you will need a 7⅛" x 5⅛" piece of fabric for pillow backing, 2" x 22½" bias fabric strip for cording, 22½" length of ¼" dia. purchased cord, and polyester fiberfill.

Centering design, trim stitched piece to measure 7⅛" x 5⅛".

Center cord on wrong side of bias strip; matching long edges, fold strip over cord. Use a zipper foot to baste along length of strip close to cord; trim seam allowance to ½". Matching raw edges, pin cording to right side of stitched piece, making a ⅜" clip in seam allowance of cording at corners. Ends of cording should overlap approximately 2"; pin overlapping end out of the way. Starting 2" from beginning end of cording and ending 4" from overlapping end, baste cording to stitched piece. On overlapping end of cording, remove 2½" of basting; fold end of fabric back and trim cord so that it meets beginning end of cord. Fold end of fabric under ½"; wrap fabric over beginning end of cording. Finish basting cording to stitched piece.

Matching right sides and leaving an opening for turning, use a ½" seam allowance to sew stitched piece and backing fabric together. Trim seam allowances diagonally at corners; turn pillow right side out carefully pushing corners outward. Stuff pillow with polyester fiberfill and blind stitch opening closed.

GENERAL INSTRUCTIONS

WORKING WITH CHARTS

How to Read Charts: Each of the designs is shown in chart form. Each colored square on the chart represents one Cross Stitch or one Half Cross Stitch. Each colored triangle on the chart represents one One-Quarter Stitch or one Three-Quarter Stitch. Black or colored dots represent French Knots or bead placement. Colored ovals represent Lazy Daisy Stitches. The black or colored straight lines on the chart indicate Backstitch. When a French Knot, Lazy Daisy Stitch, or Backstitch covers a square, the symbol is omitted.

Each chart is accompanied by a color key. This key indicates the color of floss to use for each stitch on the chart. The headings on the color key are for Cross Stitch (**X**), DMC color number (**DMC**), One-Quarter Stitch (**¼X**), Three-Quarter Stitch (**¾X**), Half Cross Stitch (**½X**), and Backstitch (**B'ST**). Color key columns should be read vertically and horizontally to determine type of stitch and floss color.

Where to Start: The horizontal and vertical centers of each charted design are shown by arrows. You may start at any point on the charted design, but be sure the design will be centered on the fabric. Locate the center of fabric by folding in half, top to bottom and again left to right. On the charted design, count the number of squares (stitches) from the center of the chart to where you wish to start. Then from the fabric's center, find your starting point by counting out the same number of fabric threads (stitches). (**Note:** To work over two fabric threads, count out twice the number of fabric threads.)

How To Determine Finished Size: The finished size of your design will depend on the **thread count per inch** of the fabric being used. To determine the finished size of the design on different fabrics, divide the number of squares (stitches) in the width of the charted design by the thread count of the fabric. For example, a charted design with a width of 80 squares worked on 14 count Aida will yield a design 5¾" wide. Repeat for the number of squares (stitches) in the height of the charted design. (**Note:** To work over two fabric threads, divide the number of squares by one-half the thread count.) Then add the amount of background you want plus a generous amount for finishing. Whipstitch or zigzag stitch the edges of your fabric to prevent raveling.

For ease in determining finished sizes on some common fabric counts, use the table below. In the left-hand column, find the approximate number of stitches in the width or height of the charted design. Follow the line across the column to find the design size under the appropriate fabric count.

THREAD COUNT PER INCH OF FABRIC		14	16	18	22
NUMBER OF STITCHES IN DESIGN (Width or Height)	10	¾	⅝	⅝	½
	20	1½	1¼	1⅛	1
	30	2¼	1⅞	1¾	1⅜
	40	2⅞	2½	2¼	1⅞
	50	3⅝	3⅛	2⅞	2⅜
	60	4⅜	3¾	3⅜	2¾
	70	5	4⅞	4	3¼
	80	5¾	5	4½	3¾
	90	6½	5⅝	5	4⅛
	100	7¼	6¼	5⅝	4⅝

Number of Strands: The number of strands of floss to use depends primarily on the count of the fabric being used. You may wish to vary the number of strands in some areas of the design to achieve different textures. Feel free to experiment with the number of strands to achieve the look you desire. You may want to try a few stitches on the corner of your fabric to see if the floss is adequately covering the fabric. For recommended number of strands to use on some common fabric counts, see the table below.

Thread Count Per Inch of Fabric	Number of Strands		
	Cross Stitch	Half Cross	Backstitch
14	2 or 3	1	1
16	2	1	1
18	2	1	1
22	1	1	1

Cut the floss you are using into 18" lengths. To ensure smoother stitches, separate the strands and realign them before threading the needle.

Selecting Needles: The tapestry needle should be large enough to be easily threaded with the number of strands of floss you are using. It should also be small enough to keep from distorting the fabric as it goes between the threads. Very little pressure is needed to push the tapestry needle between the fabric threads, so it is unnecessary to use a thimble. For recommended needle sizes on some common fabric counts, see the table below.

Thread Count Per Inch of Fabric	Tapestry Needle Size
14	24
16	24 or 26
18	26
22	26

BEGINNING FIRST STITCH

Working Over Beginning Stitches Meth
Bring needle up for first stitch. Pull fl through fabric, leaving approximately 1 floss on back of fabric. Hold floss end in p with non-stitching fingers and work sev stitches over the floss on back of fab (**Fig. 1**).

Fig. 1

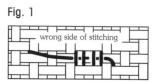
wrong side of stitching

Loop Method (can only be used with an e number of strands): Cut a 36" length of flc If stitching with 2 strands of floss, fold c 36" strand in half (for 4 strands, fold t 36" strands; for 6 strands fold th 36" strands) and thread loose ends throu needle. Bring needle up for first stitch, leav the loop on back of fabric. Make the first hal first Cross Stitch and pass the needle throu loop (**Fig. 2**). Pull floss through the loop u loop is snug against the back of fabric. Br the needle up for second half of stitch.

Fig. 2

Waste Knot Method: To make a waste knc tie a knot in end of floss, begin on the front fabric; go down through fabric 2"-3" from fi stitch and come up for first stitc (**Fig. 3**). When finished with length of flos clip knot from end of floss; thread flos through needle and run it under sever stitches on back of work.

Fig. 3

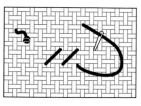

FINISHING A LENGTH OF FLOSS

Bring floss through to back of fabric t complete last stitch. Run floss under severc stitches on back of work. Clip floss close t fabric. When some of the design has beer stitched, begin stitching by running needl under several stitches on the back of work never tie knots.

TCH DIAGRAMS

e: Bring threaded needle up at 1 and
odd numbers and down at 2 and all
n numbers.

nted Cross Stitch (X): Work one Cross
ch to correspond to each colored square
the chart. For horizontal rows, work
ches in two journeys (Fig. 4). For vertical
s, complete each stitch as shown
g. 5). When working over two fabric
eads, work Cross Stitch as shown in
. 6. When the chart shows a Backstitch
ssing a colored square (Fig. 7), a Cross
ch should be worked first; then the
ckstitch (Fig. 12 or 13) should be worked
op of the Cross Stitch.

Fig. 4

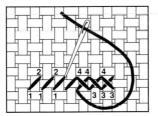

Fig. 5

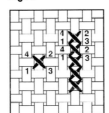

Fig. 6

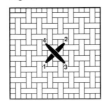

Fig.7

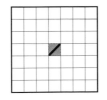

Quarter Stitch (¼X and ¾X): Quarter
Stitches are denoted by triangular shapes of
color on the chart and on the color key. For
One-Quarter Stitch, come up at 1 (Fig. 8);
then split fabric thread to go down at
2. When stitches 1-4 are worked in the same
color, the resulting stitch is called a Three-
Quarter Stitch (¾X). Fig. 9 shows the
technique for Quarter Stitches when working
over two fabric threads.

Fig. 8

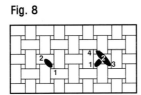

Fig. 9

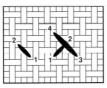

Half Cross Stitch (½X): This stitch is one
journey of the Cross Stitch and is worked
from lower left to upper right as shown in
Fig. 10. When working over two fabric
threads, work Half Cross Stitch as shown in
Fig. 11.

Fig. 10

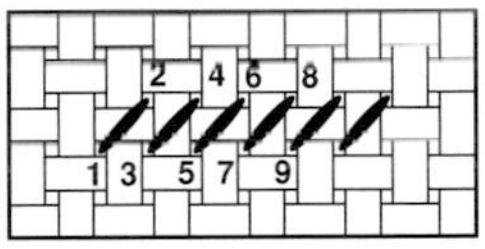

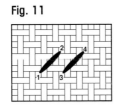

Fig. 11

Backstitch (B'ST): For outline detail,
Backstitch (shown on chart and on color key
by black or colored straight lines) should be
worked after the design has been completed
(Fig. 12). When working over two fabric
threads, work Backstitch as shown in
Fig. 13.

Fig. 12

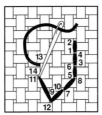

Fig. 13

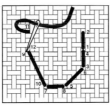

French Knot: Bring needle up at 1. Wrap floss
once around needle and insert needle at 2,
holding end of floss with non-stitching fingers
(Fig. 14). Tighten knot; then pull needle
through fabric, holding floss until it must be
released. For larger knot, use more strands;
wrap only once.

Fig. 14

Lazy Daisy Stitch: Bring needle up at 1 and
make a loop. Go down at 1 and come up at
2, keeping floss below point of needle
(Fig. 15). Pull needle through and go down
at 2 to anchor loop, completing stitch.
(Note: To support stitches, it may be helpful
to go down in edge of next fabric thread
when anchoring loop.)

Fig. 15

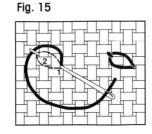

Continued on page 94.

STITCHING TIPS

Working Over Two Fabric Threads: Use the sewing method instead of the stab method when working over two fabric threads. To use the sewing method, keep your stitching hand on the right side of the fabric (instead of stabbing the fabric with the needle and taking your stitching hand to the back of the fabric to pick up the needle). With the sewing method, you take the needle down and up with one stroke instead of two. To add support to stitches, it is important that the first Cross Stitch is placed on the fabric with stitch 1-2 beginning and ending where a vertical fabric thread crosses over a horizontal fabric thread (**Fig. 16**). When the first stitch is in the correct position, the entire design will be placed properly, with vertical fabric threads supporting each stitch.

Fig. 16

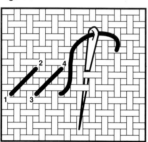

Working On Perforated Paper: Perforated paper has a right side and a wrong side. The right side is smoother and stitching should be done on this side. To find the center, do not fold paper; use a ruler and mark lightly with a pencil or count holes. Perforated paper will tear if handled roughly; therefore, hold the paper flat while stitching and do not use a hoop. Begin and end stitching by running floss under several stitches on back; never tie knots. Use the stab method when stitching and keep stitching tension consistent. Thread pulled too tightly may tear the paper. Carry floss across back as little as possible.

Attaching Beads: Refer to chart for bead placement and sew bead in place using a fine needle that will pass through bead. Bring needle up at 1, run needle through bead then down at 2. Secure floss on back or move to next bead as shown in **Fig. 17**.

Fig. 17

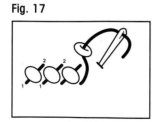

Working On Waste Canvas: Waste canvas is a special canvas that provides an evenweave grid for placing stitches on fabric. After the design is worked over the canvas, the canvas threads are removed leaving the design on the fabric. The canvas is available in several mesh sizes.

Cover edges of canvas with masking tape. Cut a piece of lightweight non-fusible interfacing the same size as canvas to provide a firm stitching base.

Find desired stitching area and mark center of area with a pin. Match center of canvas to pin. Use the blue threads in canvas to place canvas straight on garment; pin canvas to garment. Pin interfacing to wrong side of garment. Baste all layers together as shown in **Fig. 18**.

Using a sharp needle, work design, stitching from large holes to large holes. Trim canvas to within $3/4$" of design. Dampen canvas until it becomes limp. Pull out canvas threads one at a time using tweezers (**Fig. 19**). Trim interfacing close to design.

Fig. 18

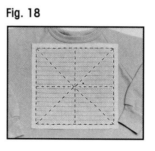

Fig. 19

PILLOW FINISHING

Love Pillow Finishing (shown on page 37, chart and supplies on page 73): Center cord on wrong side of bias strip; matching long edges, fold strip over cord. Use a zipper foot to baste along length of strip close to cord; trim seam allowance to $1/2$". Matching raw edges, pin cording to right side of stitched piece and make a $3/8$" clip in seam allowance of cording at corners. Ends of cording should overlap approximately 2"; pin overlapping end out of way. Starting 2" from beginning end of cording and ending 4" from overlapping end, baste cording to stitched piece. On overlapping end of cording, remove $2 1/2$" of basting; fold end of bias strip back and trim cord so that it meets beginning end of cord. Fold end of bias strip $1/2$" to wrong side; wrap bias strip over beginning end of cording. Finish basting cording to stitched piece.

For lace ruffle, press short edges of l $1/2$" to wrong side. Matching raw edge stitched piece and bound edge of lace, mac baste through all layers $1/2$" from edges. B stitch pressed edges together.

Matching right sides and leaving an oper for turning, use a $1/2$" seam allowance to stitched piece and backing fabric together. seam allowances diagonally at corners; pillow right side out carefully pushing cor outward. Stuff pillow with polyester fiberfill blind stitch opening closed.

SACHET FINISHING

Heart Sachet Finishing (shown on page chart and supplies on page 72): Center cord wrong side of bias strip; matching long edg fold strip over cord. Use a zipper foot to ba along length of strip close to cord; trim se allowance to $1/2$". Matching raw edges, cording to right side of stitched piece and me a $3/8$" clip in seam allowance of cording corners. Ends of cording should over approximately $1 1/4$"; pin overlapping end out way. Starting $1 3/8$" from beginning end cording and ending $1 1/2$" from overlapping e baste cording to stitched piece. On overlapp end of cording, remove $1 3/8$" of basting; fold e of bias strip back and trim cord so that it me beginning end of cord. Fold end of bias st $3/8$" to wrong side; wrap bias strip ov beginning end of cording. Finish basti cording to stitched piece.

Matching right sides and leaving an openi for turning, use a $1/2$" seam allowance to s stitched piece and backing fabric together. Tr seam allowances to $1/4$" and trim diagonally corners; turn sachet right side out, careful pushing corners outward. Stuff sachet w polyester fiberfill; place a few drops of scent oil on a small amount of polyester fiberfill. Ins scented fiberfill in middle of sachet and bli stitch opening closed.

"Two Hearts One Love" Sachet Finishir (shown on page 37, chart and supplies o page 72): Center cord on wrong side of bio strip; matching long edges, fold strip over cor Use a zipper foot to baste along length of str close to cord; trim seam allowance to $1/$ Matching raw edges, pin cording to right side stitched piece and make a $3/8$" clip in sear allowance of cording at corners. Ends cording should overlap approximately $1 1/4$"; p overlapping end out of way. Starting $1 3/8$" fror beginning end of cording and ending $1 1/2$" fror overlapping end, baste cording to stitche piece. On overlapping end of cording, remov $1 3/8$" of basting; fold end of bias strip back an trim cord so that it meets beginning end of cor Fold end of bias strip $3/8$" to wrong side; wra bias strip over beginning end of cording. Finis basting cording to stitched piece.

Matching right sides and leaving an opening turning, use a 1/2" seam allowance to sew [stit]ched piece and backing fabric together. Trim [se]am allowances to 1/4" and trim diagonally at [co]rners; turn sachet right side out, carefully [pu]shing corners outward. Stuff sachet with [po]lyester fiberfill; place a few drops of scented [oil] on a small amount of polyester fiberfill. Insert [sc]ented fiberfill in middle of sachet and blind [sti]tch opening closed.

[D]OUBLE HEMSTITCH INSTRUCTIONS

[Ta]ble Runner Finishing (shown on page 16, [ch]art on pages 54-55): Measure 1 1/4" from one [sh]ort edge of fabric and withdraw next [4] fabric threads. Turn fabric 1/4" to wrong side [an]d press; turn 1/2" to wrong side again. Folded [ed]ge of hem should be at outside edge of [wi]thdrawn area.

Working from right to left on **wrong** side of [fa]bric, secure one strand of ecru floss at edge of [fa]bric on outside edge of withdrawn area. Bring [ne]edle behind 4 fabric threads in the withdrawn [ar]ea (**Fig. 20**). Bring needle behind same fabric [th]reads a second time and come up with needle [th]rough fabric catching folded edge (**Fig. 21**); firmly pull on floss. Bring needle [be]hind 4 fabric threads for each stitch, continue [in] the same manner across withdrawn area. (If [n]umber of threads in withdrawn area is not [d]ivisible by 4, adjust number of threads used in [l]ast 2 stitches as needed.) Turn fabric and [r]epeat to work hemstitch along inside edge of [w]ithdrawn area; bring needle behind same [fa]bric threads as stitch worked on opposite [e]dge of withdrawn area as shown in **Fig. 22**. [R]epeat for remaining short edge of fabric.

Fig. 20

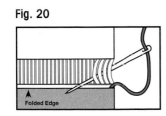

Fig. 21

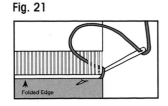

Fig. 22

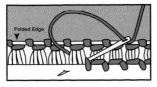

Napkin Finishing (shown on page 16, chart on page 55): Measure 1" from one raw edge of fabric and withdraw next 3 fabric threads. Turn fabric 5/8" to wrong side, press and unfold. Repeat for each side.

To miter corners, fold each corner diagonally to the wrong side until fold lines on right and wrong sides of fabric (pink and blue lines of **Fig. 23**) are matched. Trim off corner 1/4" from folded edge (dotted line of **Fig. 23**). Fold remaining raw edges 1/4" to wrong side; press. Following first fold lines and mitering corners (**Fig. 24**), fold hem 3/8" to wrong side and pin in place; folded edge of hem should be at outside edge of withdrawn area.

Working from right to left on **wrong** side of fabric, secure one strand of ecru floss at edge of fabric on outside edge of withdrawn area. Bring needle behind 4 fabric threads of right side of fabric and 4 fabric threads of hem in the withdrawn area (**Fig. 25**). Bring needle behind same fabric threads a second time and come up with needle through fabric as shown in **Fig. 26**; firmly pull on floss.

Fig. 23

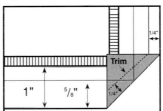

Fig. 24

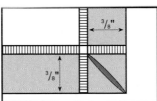

Fig. 25

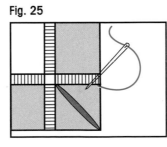

Fig. 26

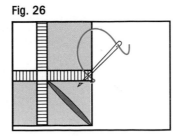

Continue in same manner to intersection of withdrawn areas. Bring needle behind 4 fabric threads of fabric; bring needle behind same fabric threads a second time and come up with needle through fabric catching folded edge (**Fig. 27**); firmly pull on floss. Continue in same manner to next intersection of withdrawn areas. (If number of threads in withdrawn area is not divisible by 4, adjust number of threads used in last 2 stitches as needed.) Bring needle behind 4 fabric threads of right side of fabric and 4 fabric threads of hem in the withdrawn area. Bring needle behind same fabric threads a second time and come up with needle through fabric; firmly pull on floss. Continue in same manner to left edge of fabric. Turn fabric and repeat to work hemstitch along inside edge of withdrawn area; bring needle behind same fabric threads as stitch worked on opposite edge of withdrawn area as shown in **Fig. 28**. Repeat for remaining edges of fabric.

Fig. 27

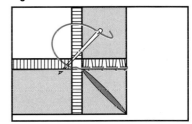

Fig. 28

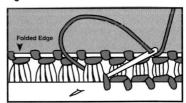

Instructions tested and photo items made by Janet Akins, Lisa Arey, Kandi Ashford, Marsha Besancon, Vicky Bishop, Karen Brogan, Carrie Clifford, Alice Crowder, Vanessa Edwards, Jody Fuller, Joyce Graves, Nelwyn Gray, Muriel Hicks, Diana Hoke, Joyce Holland, Vanessa Kiihnl, Melanie Long, Phyllis Lundy, Susan McDonald, Colleen Moline, Margaret Moseley, Ray Ellen Odle, Patricia O'Neil, Susan Sego, Lavonne Sims, Amy Taylor, Trish Vines, Jane Walker, Ruth White, and Marie Williford.